Giuseppe Frassinetti, Lady Georgiana Chatterton

The Consolation of the devout Soul

an appendix on the holy fear of God

Giuseppe Frassinetti, Lady Georgiana Chatterton

The Consolation of the devout Soul
an appendix on the holy fear of God

ISBN/EAN: 9783337815998

Printed in Europe, USA, Canada, Australia, Japan

Cover: Foto ©Lupo / pixelio.de

More available books at **www.hansebooks.com**

THE CONSOLATION

OF THE

DEVOUT SOUL.

BY THE
VERY REV. JOSEPH FRASSINETTI,
PRIOR OF ST. SABINA, IN GENOA.

WITH AN

𝔄𝔭𝔭𝔢𝔫𝔡𝔦𝔵 𝔬𝔫 𝔱𝔥𝔢 𝔥𝔬𝔩𝔶 𝔉𝔢𝔞𝔯 𝔬𝔣 𝔊𝔬𝔡.

TRANSLATED BY GEORGIANA LADY CHATTERTON.

LONDON: BURNS AND OATES,
Portman Street and Paternoster Row.
1876.

Imprimatur.

✠ **GULIELMUS BERNARDUS,**
Episcopus Birminghamiensis.

Dec. 1876.

PREFACE TO THE ENGLISH TRANSLATION.

IN offering this translation to the Catholic public of England, I have a few words to say about the cause and manner of its appearance at this time. They shall be as few as possible, but the reader will see that they are necessary. No sooner had my most beloved and lamented wife become a Catholic than, with that thoroughness of purpose and purity of intention which characterised her whole life, she at once desired to write something definitely Catholic. The first thing she wrote in pursuance of that object was a pamphlet called *Convictions*, addressed to Protestant friends, as a corrective sequel to one she had previously written under the name of *Misgivings*. She then began two works, an original story (which, in consequence of her death, is in every way but a fragment of what it would have been) and this translation. I publish the translation first, because I know that she would have done so herself; but both would have been brought out long ago if I had been capable of giving practical attention to anything. Had it been the Will of Almighty God that she should recover her health, she would have done very great service to Catholic literature; but He ruled it otherwise. May His most holy Will be done!

EDWARD HENEAGE DERING.

Baddesley Clinton, November 1876.

To Mary,

WHO IS THE MOTHER OF BEAUTIFUL LOVE, OF FEAR, AND KNOWLEDGE AND HOLY HOPE.

THOU, O Mary, art the Mother of beautiful love, because thou dost infuse pure and holy love—love of the Infinite Beauty, which is God—into the hearts of thy children. Thou art the Mother of that chaste fear which takes away all fear but that of not being sufficiently pure in the eyes of God. Thou art the Mother of that heavenly knowledge which entirely fills their minds with the light of God, so that they recognise Him to be the only true Good. Thou art the Mother of that blessed hope, through which, abandoning themselves entirely to Him, they have in this life a foretaste of eternal peace. Thou art therefore the fountain of Christian devotion, which is nothing else but the ardour of heavenly love, the quiet fear of a filial tenderness, the living light of the Divine Wisdom, and the consolation of secure hope.

To thee I again recommend this my little work, to the end that it may conduce to the increase of true devotion. If thou wilt console with thine ineffable grace every devout soul into whose hands it may fall, I am certain that it will attain the end for which it is intended.

PREFACE BY THE AUTHOR.

REFLECTING on the number of souls who hold the most pernicious error, that sanctity or Christian perfection is something excessively difficult to acquire, I felt, as it were, spurred on to write this little book, for the purpose of undeceiving them.

Yes, indeed, it is a most pernicious error; for these souls, as if terror-struck at the supposed difficulty of obtaining their own sanctification, neglect their own part in the matter, and, instead of becoming holy, remain in their state of imperfection and sin.

I wish this little book to suit all capacities, for God wills that all should be holy; and in every condition, every state of life, there are people to be found, I think, who are in need of some light—or, more correctly speaking, of some attention and reflection—on the facility of arriving at sanctification. I have therefore taken care that it should be very plain and simple, adapted to those who are least cultivated and dullest of apprehension, who cannot read voluminous treatises, and have no capacity for subtle conceptions. I have entitled it *The Consolation of the Devout Soul,* because my words are addressed to the devout; and I believe that there is no better way to encourage these in the way of perfection than by convincing them that it is not too difficult of attainment. And if any one should be inclined to suspect from this that I have not considered those words of our Saviour (St. Matt. vii. 14), 'Quam angusta porta et arcta est via quæ ducit ad vitam,'—' How narrow is the gate, and strait is the way, which leadeth to life,' that is, to Paradise,—let him understand that I have considered them well, and have observed that it is the enemies of the Church who understand our Lord's words in the sense of its being excessively difficult and sometimes impossible to enter by that gate and walk in the way which leads to Heaven. With St. John Chrysostom, I understand, in the Catholic sense, that this gate and this road are narrow, not for devout souls, but for worldly and sensual people, who will not keep their passions under restraint. It is necessary to understand them in this sense, or we should have to say that they contradict those other words of Christ, 'My yoke is sweet, and My burden is light,' which would be blasphemy. (See Maldonato on this text.)

In the mean while I beg the reader to consider well what my aim is. My aim is not to write a treatise on Christian perfection—the small size of this volume would of itself make this evident, but only to undeceive those who see too many difficulties in the way of its attainment. Hoping, then, that a few souls the more may determine on aspiring to it when their misapprehension shall have been removed, I add something on its beauty and on two means of arriving at it, which are among the most necessary, and which I judge to be the most opportune. For the rest, whatever is wanting will be supplied to those who can read, and are able to employ themselves in literary occupations, by the excellent books we have on the subject, and to those who cannot, by the wise instruction of their directors. I consider this notice to be necessary, lest my work should unjustly be reputed insufficient, and hence be disapproved.

I have added, as suitable to the object I have in view, an Appendix on the tranquillity and confidence that ought to accompany the holy fear of God.

This is the ninth edition known to me; others have been brought out here and there that I have not seen. The text that will be followed is that of the sixth edition, added to and corrected by myself, and again looked over since.

CONTENTS.

CHAPTER I.

SECT.   PAGE

1. The precise idea of Christian sanctity.   . .   1
2. Lays down what it is that we have to do in order to accomplish the Will of God   . . .   1
3. Distinguishes two kinds of holiness   . . .   2
4. Shows that a soul purified from mortal sin really is a holy soul   2
5. Explains what it is that is requisite for the attainment of Christian perfection.   . . .   5
6. Shows that we should all tend towards Christian perfection.   8

CHAPTER II.

SHOWS THAT CHRISTIAN PERFECTION IS NOT A THING TOO DIFFICULT TO BE ACQUIRED, p. 9.

1. Distinguishes two kinds of venial sin   . . .   9
2. That faults committed quite inadvertently are by no means to be called sins   10
3. Determines what kinds of venial sin are an impediment to perfect union with the Divine Will   .   13
4. Shows that it is not too difficult for us to avoid venial sins   14

SECT.   PAGE
5. That, in itself it is an easier thing to avoid venial sins of which we are fully aware than it is to avoid mortal sin 15
6. Why it is easier to fall into mortal than into venial sins 17
7. That it is not too difficult for us to seek what is most pleasing to God in things that are themselves indifferent 19

CHAPTER III.

THE DIFFICULTIES USUALLY BROUGHT AGAINST THE ABOVE-MENTIONED DOCTRINES ARE SOLVED, p. 22.

1. That it is not necessary to practise the evangelical counsels in order to attain Christian perfection 22
2. For the attainment of Christian Perfection extraordinary favours are not required . . . 23
3. That God desires the greater part of mankind to be holy for their own sake; and only some for themselves and for others 26
4. That we cannot aspire to be chosen by God as sublime examples of holiness 31
5. Gives the example of saints who through humility regretted having extraordinary gifts . 32
6. Conclusion of the answer to objections . . 34
7. That human weakness does not render the attainment of Christian perfection too difficult . . 36
8. That the truly humble should not lose confidence on account of their own weakness . . . 39
9. That bad natural dispositions cannot make it too difficult to acquire Christian perfection . . 42
10. Shows that it is not too difficult for us to gain the necessary power of self-denial . . . 53
11. Nor is it too difficult to seek in all things what is most pleasing to God 57

SECT.		PAGE
12.	Neither can the perils of the world nor family cares hinder our sanctification . . .	61
13.	Shows that business and laborious work, family cares, and all the other occupations consequent on our condition in life, may be made to assist us greatly in the attainment of Christian perfection	63
14.	That albeit we are unworthy, we ought to hope for the grace of sanctity .· . . .	65

CHAPTER IV.

THE BEAUTY AND UTILITY OF CHRISTIAN PERFECTION, p. 69.

1. The beauty of Christian perfection . . . 69
2. The multifarious ways in which Christian perfection is useful. First, in the testimony of a good conscience 71
3. Secondly, in the greater security of being in a state of grace 72
4. Thirdly, the greater security of not losing the grace of God 75
5. Fourthly, the special favour with which God regards those who aspire to Christian perfection . 77

CHAPTER V.

ON THE MEANS OF ARRIVING AT THIS MUCH-DESIRED CHRISTIAN PERFECTION, p. 80.

1. The first thing to be done in order to attain Christian perfection is to desire it 80
2. This desire should be a resolve, and put immediately into practice 81
3. That we should not relax our efforts because we have not succeeded hitherto 85

SECT.		PAGE
4.	That prayer insures the efficacy of the good desire	87
5.	That the second thing to be done is to have a good spiritual director	89
6.	Digression on the encouragement that this doctrine gives to devout souls	92
7.	Necessity of obedience to one's spiritual director	100
8.	That it is not too difficult a thing to find a good spiritual director, and that if we do not, God will supply the need	103
9.	When among various directors a selection can be made, we ought to choose one of the best; and suggestions are made for instruction on this head	106
10.	Prototype of a good director	110
	Conclusion	113

APPENDIX.

WHAT SORT OF IDEA THE DEVOUT SOUL SHOULD TAKE CARE TO HAVE ABOUT THE HOLY FEAR OF GOD, p. 115.

1.	The holy fear of God should be a calm and tranquil fear	117
2.	When the fear of God is not tranquil it impedes what is good, and may do much evil	118
3.	On the means of preserving tranquillity of heart	120
4.	We ought not to lose tranquillity of heart because we commit faults and even sins	126
5.	We ought not to lose tranquillity of heart on account of the uncertainty of our remaining in a state of grace	127
6.	Neither should we lose tranquillity from a dread of hidden mortal sin	130
7.	Nor from fear that we may not have well repented of the sins of our past life	134

CONTENTS.

SECT. | PAGE
8. Nor ought we to lose confidence from the fear of having consented to wicked thoughts . . 140
9. Neither should the continual danger of falling into sin cause us to lose our inward tranquillity 149
10. The holy fear of God ought to be full of confidence 157
Conclusion 163

NOTES.

NO.
1. 170
2. On moderation in explaining maxims of terror . 170
3. The facility of making an act of the perfect love of God 176
4. Zeal for the salvation of souls among secular persons 178

ON THE CAUSES AND EFFECTS OF TRIBULATION . 182
TRIBULATION IS A SIGN OF PREDESTINATION . . 189

The Consolation of the Devout Soul.

CHAPTER I.

§ 1. *On the precise idea of Christian sanctity.*

ALL holy persons agree that Christian sanctity consists in charity—that is, in the fulfilment of the Divine Will; so that a soul which executes the Divine Will is a holy soul: and the better this is carried out the more holy is the soul.

Of the truth of this doctrine one cannot doubt, and no spiritual teacher has ever doubted it.

Remember, then, O devout soul, in whatever state and condition you find yourself, that if you strive to follow the Will of God you are holy, and that the more you try to carry it out perfectly the more holy will you be.

§ 2. *Lays down what it is we have to do in order to accomplish the Will of God.*

But what is required, you will ask, to fulfil the

Holy Will of God? I answer, nothing more and nothing less than the observance of the commandments of God's law, and of the Church which commands us by Divine authority. If you fulfil well these commandments you accomplish the Holy Will of God, and by this you are holy. Such is the doctrine of St. Thomas, the angelic doctor (2—2, q. 184, a. 3).

§ 3. *Distinguishes two kinds of holiness.*

But we should distinguish two kinds of holiness. The first is simple sanctity, which consists in the possession of sanctifying grace; and this all souls possess that are pure from mortal sin. The second is sanctity perfected; and this consists in the perfect union of our will with the Will of God; so that the soul abhors not only mortal sin, but also deliberate venial sins, and is ready to execute that which we clearly know to be the most pleasing to God, even in things which are not expressly commanded. (St. Thomas, 2—2, q. 184, a. 2.)

§ 4. *Shows that a soul free from mortal sin really is a holy soul.*

In the first place, it is true holiness to keep the soul pure from mortal sin, even though it be stained with venial sins. And this is truly of faith; because the soul which is not guilty of mortal sin has sanctifying grace, which grace is named sanctifying precisely because it is the cause of sanctification, and is a gift of God inherent in the soul, rendering her the friend of God, the daughter of God, sister to our Lord Jesus Christ, heir of Paradise, and in consequence really holy. Hence it is to be observed that by this grace are holy even the blessed in Heaven, as also the great Mother of God herself, the most holy Mary; so that if they were to lose the sanctifying grace of God (which is not possible) even in Heaven they would be no longer saints. Therefore, as St. Thomas teaches, this grace is in some sort a beginning of the glory that we shall receive in Heaven (2—2, q. 243); and that light of glory, by which the souls in Heaven see God with clearness, is nothing but the same grace arrived at its total completeness. Therefore the soul that has never sinned mortally against the law of God or of the Church, or, should it indeed have done so, has obtained pardon by means of the necessary repentance, such a soul possesses real holiness, though it may have defects and venial sins, since these do not deprive it of sanctifying grace. Clearly, then, they are in error who think that those souls only are good and holy who give indications of singular perfection, and that others who have no mortal sins, but frequently fall into defects and failings, are neither saintly nor good. Yet this does not mean (it must be remembered) that venial sins are to be treated lightly; on the contrary, as we shall see, we should consider them of great importance. But I wish clearly to make known the preciousness of sanctifying grace, which of itself constitutes a most happy state—that in which man enjoys the true friendship of God, and in which, if we are surprised by death in any way, it is impossible to lose Paradise.

How desirable it is that Christians should know well the preciousness of this gift of God! They would certainly make much more account of it, and they would not so lightly run the risk of losing it, as now they sometimes do. Oh, what a most precious ore this is, although sometimes found in a soul alloyed with many imperfections and defects! Oh, what a pearl, what a gem, although not yet purified and polished! People take little care of the richest jewel if they are not fully aware of its worth, and they easily allow it to be stolen by thieves; but if they are aware of its value, they defend it so zealously that neither skill nor violence on the part of the thief will avail to rob them of it. I could wish that all preachers and confessors and writers of spiritual books would undertake, as their principal employment, that of making known to Christians the preciousness of sanctifying grace.

§ 5. *Explains what it is that is requisite for the attainment of Christian perfection.*

This sanctity however is a simple holiness, and has its own intrinsic good without the perfection which it ought to have, as gold just taken out of the earth is true gold and precious, but is full of alloy, and has not the beautiful splendour which it afterwards acquires when purified. And therefore perfect sanctity is generally called Christian perfection, which consists not only in the possession of sanctifying grace, but also in the most perfect union of the soul's will with the Will of God. This perfect sanctity those souls possess who, disengaging themselves from every inordinate attachment to creatures, live resolved never to commit anything displeasing to God, and in everything are ready to do whatsoever they clearly know to be pleasing to Him. For this reason they cautiously guard themselves against venial sins, and in things which are not expressly commanded or prohibited by the laws of God and the Church apply themselves always to do that which they see to be most conformable to God's pleasure. We say, '*when they know* God's Will *clearly*,' because we well know in general what are the things that God loves most in themselves; but often we do not know in particular what pleases Him with regard to us. For example, we know that poverty is pleasing to God, and that to renounce all the goods of this life is pleasing to Him, as St. Francis of Assisi did, who deprived himself of everything; but we do not know whether it would be pleasing to God that this renouncement should be made by us or by any other particular person. In the same manner, we know it to be pleasing to God that all Christians should hear Mass daily, even on weekdays; but we do not know whether He wishes us or any other particular person to hear Mass every day, when, owing to family circumstances or necessary works, it is fitting that we should do so, in general, on festivals only.

What we ought to do, if we wish to be holy and perfect as far as it is possible to be so in this life, is this: we must guard ourselves not only from mortal sins, but also from venial ones, by resolving never consciously to commit any, from any motive or cause whatsoever; and also in everything we must endeavour to do what is most pleasing to God so far as we know. In this way we shall be pure from all inordinate affections to creatures; we shall have our wills fully conformed to the Will of God; and, in a word, we shall be saintly and perfect. I said indeed, 'as far as we can be so in this life,' because, as St. Augustine teaches, a perfection absolutely complete is reserved for us in Paradise, and no one has ever possessed it among the pure in this world except the Blessed Virgin Mary. For which reason St. Bernard said that the continual striving after perfection is accounted for perfection in this mortal life: 'Jugis conatus ad perfectionem perfectio reputatur,'—' A continual striving after perfection is considered perfection.' And remember that as perfect sanctity consists in the perfect union of our wills with the Will of God, it consists in the perfect love of God; for there is no doubt that two persons love each other perfectly when there is between them a perfect union of will, forming between the two one single heart. Now when our heart is resolved to desire nothing but what the heart of God desires, it becomes united in such a manner with the same that it forms almost one heart; and thus between us and God there is true love, and the perfection of love.

§ 6. *Shows that we should all tend towards Christian perfection.*

This perfect sanctity is without doubt what God desires in all Christians; in fact, who would dare to say that God permits us to commit venial sins, and will be contented that we should prefer our own will and pleasure to His, leaving undone what we clearly know to be His pleasure? A master will not endure to receive from his servant serious injuries and wrongs, but neither will he be at all content to receive small annoyances from him. A master insists that his servant shall obey him in those things which he absolutely commands, but he also wishes him to carry out any unexpressed desire; and consequently that servant only is considered the best who takes care not to cause his master knowingly any, even the very least, displeasure, and who endeavours to satisfy his desires in all things. Could we imagine that our most wise and most just Master will be content with less? No. This sanctity is certainly the only kind that fully satisfies God, and renders the soul perfect. To this I exhort you, and I propose to show you that it is not too difficult of attainment.

CHAPTER II.

THAT CHRISTIAN PERFECTION IS NOT A THING TOO DIFFICULT TO BE ACQUIRED.

SINCE, for the fulfilment of Christian perfection, we only require perfect union with the Divine Will, and in order to have this union we need do nothing more than avoid sin, even venial ones, and endeavour in all things neither prohibited nor enjoined to do what is most pleasing to God, it is necessary for me to show you that it is not too difficult a thing to attain this Christian perfection or perfect union with the Divine Will : it is necessary for me to show you that it is not too difficult to avoid even venial sins, and to seek in all things that which is most pleasing to God. But with regard to venial sins I must first lay down a most necessary distinction.

§ 1. *Distinguishes two kinds of venial sins.*

We should notice that there are venial sins of which we are fully conscious—that is, those which we commit with open eyes, knowing clearly that we are doing wrong at the moment; as, for instance, if we are aware that we tell a falsehood in order to excuse some ill-advised action, and in the mean time we tell it, knowing the malice of that falsehood; or if we are aware that such and such a recital may even lightly injure the good fame of our neighbour, and yet, knowing the malice of mentioning it, we do not refrain from doing so. On the other hand, there are venial sins of which we are not fully aware, and which we commit more from weakness than malice, such as certain distractions in prayer, or some useless words or impatient actions, and similar errors into which we fall without being well aware of them.

§ 2. *That faults committed quite inadvertently are by no means to be called sins.*

I said before, 'the errors into which we fall without being fully conscious of them;' because when there is absolutely no consciousness, and therefore no voluntary malice, they cannot be called even venial sins, but are only imperfections and weaknesses of human nature, from which we cannot in any way guard ourselves, and of which we cannot in any way repent; since, as St. Augustine says, where there is no voluntary malice there is no sin. And here I must make a little digression which appears to me important.

This truth I should wish to impress on those souls that accuse themselves of their natural weaknesses as if they were sins, and mourn over them, and believe themselves to be through them in a bad state before God, so that sometimes they even omit the Holy Communion prescribed by their own director, judging themselves to be too unworthy to receive it. How much they are in error! Do not even children know that where there is no voluntary malice there can be no sin? But these persons fancy they find sin where there is not a shadow of it, nay even where there actually is merit. If it happens that they feel a momentary impatience, or envy, or sensuality, they immediately think they have sinned, although they endeavoured to repress those feelings when as yet they were scarcely aware of them. These persons, then, have not sinned in this matter, for they cannot avoid such feelings: nay, indeed, by combating them the moment they become aware of the same they obtain merit. Hear what St. John of the Cross says: 'If you do not give your consent, but rather experience displeasure and abhorrence of them, and with patience endure them, they purify your will as fire does gold. These weaknesses, these miseries, are the necessary consequence of original sin, in the same way as diseases and other temporal ills are evils to which all the children of Adam are subject, and from which no one could pretend to be entirely free without pretending to a privilege which God does not grant.'

We must also remark and remember that this is the Catholic doctrine, as taught by the sacred Council of Trent against the errors of Protestants, who pretend that the involuntary motions of concupiscence—that is, of the sensitive appetites—are sins. On the other hand, some people may object that the masters of spirituality exhort those souls who aspire to perfection to lay bare to their directors their evil inclinations and the temptations they have to suffer: and to do this is certainly praiseworthy, because, by manifesting these things to our own director, we may learn from him the most opportune and efficacious means of conquering them. Indeed, I exhort you to lay bare to your director your whole soul—your evil inclinations, and the temptations that molest you; that is, provided he does not already know them, and has not commanded you to be silent about them; but for pity's sake do not accuse yourself of them as if they were sins; for sins they are not, and consequently are not matters for confession. For pity's sake do not be terrified by these miserable sensations, which are compatible with the most perfect sanctity that is to be found in the world. And do not tell me that the saints do not experience these miseries also; for I can answer you that no theologian is to be found who believes that any saint ever existed who did not experience at some time or other inclinations to evil, except the Queen of saints, the most holy Mary. And if there be any saint who did not experience any perverse inclination against any given virtue, it was only a special privilege, which is by no means a necessary part of sanctity. Indeed St. Aloysius Gonzaga never had the slightest temptation against holy chastity; but would you place him above the Apostle St. Paul, who suffered severely in this way?

§ 3. *Determines what kinds of venial sins are an impediment to perfect union with the Divine Will.*

The venial sins which hinder our perfect union with the Will of God, and which consequently hinder the progress of Christian perfection, are those of which we are fully aware—that is to say, those which (as I have said) we commit with our eyes open. The other venial sins, of which we are not fully aware, do not hinder the progress of Christian perfection; and these are what produce a kind of tepidity which St. Alphonsus designates as inevitable (*Pract.* cap. vii. n. 2), because the soul cannot be exempt from them without a special privilege from God, according to the teaching of the holy Council of Trent; and it is not known that any one of the saints has possessed this privilege, with the exception of the most Blessed Virgin Mary. Now then, since no one can pretend that your purity of conscience equals that of the great Mother of God, so no one can teach you that, in order to progress in Christian perfection, you must always be free even from venial sins of which you are not fully aware. Of such I am not going to speak for the present.

§ 4. *That it is not too difficult a thing for us to avoid venial sins.*

. This truth is evident from the following reason: God not only commands us absolutely to avoid mortal sin, but absolutely commands us to avoid venial sins. God forbids us to blaspheme His Sacred Name, and God forbids us even to take that

Name in vain. God forbids us to swear a false oath, and forbids us to lie for our amusement. Now can we suppose that Divine Goodness would make prohibitions too arduous and too hard for His creatures—that He could give commands too difficult for us to observe? Tyrants only have, from time to time, imposed on their subjects commands too difficult to be obeyed; but good sovereigns have never done so. Still less have good fathers done so as regards their children; and we, who confess that God is the Sovereign King, the most perfect Father of His creatures,—how can we, without doing the gravest wrong to His ineffable tenderness, suppose that He would command us to do things that are too difficult of fulfilment? If, then, we must not suppose that the Divine Goodness could impose on His creatures commands too difficult for them to observe, it is not to be supposed that to avoid venial sins is too difficult for us, since He commands us to abstain even from these.

§ 5. *That, in itself, it is an easier thing to avoid venial sins of which we are fully aware than it is to avoid mortal sin.*

And why indeed, with the assistance of Divine Grace, can we not abstain from venial sins of which we are fully conscious, as well as from mortal sin? If we are able to overcome temptations to mortal sin, which are the strongest and most violent, shall we find greater difficulty in overcoming temptations to venial sins, which are so much weaker and lighter? Shall we be able to overcome the impetuosity of certain passions, which made even the greatest saints tremble, and shall we not conquer the temptation to tell a lie, to say something slightly injurious to our neighbour's character? Samson, we are told in the Divine Scriptures, had received from God strength so prodigious that he strangled with his own hands the most tremendous lions, and broke their bones in pieces as if they had been tender little lambs. Would you, then, believe me if I were to tell you that he had not strength enough to strangle and kill a little fox? When we fight against strong temptations, by yielding to which we should commit mortal sin, we are striving against terrible lions; when, on the other hand, we fight against temptations to venial sins, we are fighting against little foxes; and, therefore, not only ought we to succeed, by the aid of Divine grace, in avoiding venial sins with the same facility as we avoid mortal sins, but we ought to overcome the former even more easily than the latter.

§ 6. *Shows that, in itself, it is an easier thing to avoid deliberate venial sin than mortal sin.*

How, then, does it happen that we, through the Divine assistance, overcome temptations to mortal sin, passing months—perhaps years, without falling into them, and meanwhile do not, so to speak, pass one day without yielding to the temptations of venial sin? This is the reason: Mortal sin, if we have but a little faith, terrifies us: the eternal hell which yawns at our feet makes us tremble. Therefore, with the Divine assistance, we immediately fight manfully against the temptation, and we overcome it. Here the lion is strangled—the lion conquered. On the other hand, venial sin appears to us no evil at all; and the purgatory which will end only frightens us as the summer heat does, which we know will soon be followed by the coolness of autumn. For this reason temptations to venial sins do not put us in any apprehension, and with the utmost facility we yield to them. This is the real reason why so many Christian souls, while they succeed in guarding themselves from mortal sins, do not also succeed in warding off venial sins. Oh, if these souls would seriously consider that even venial sin is a grievous evil because it is an offence to a Goodness which is Infinite—that is, to God! If they would but consider that it is an evil so great that no evil in this world can be compared to it; that one venial sin alone is a worse evil than if a pestilence should kill every one in the world —worse than if an earthquake should destroy all the cities on this earth; that it is a worse evil than the deluge which, in the days of Noah, drowned, with the exception of his own family, all human beings, worse than the deluge of fire which, before the universal judgment, will reduce to ashes all the world! If people would but consider seriously that purgatory is a terrible punishment from God, and so agonising that it would be better to suffer all possible earthly torments for a hundred years than have to endure purgatory for one day! If these considerations could but impress themselves on Christian souls, oh, then certainly we should seriously resolve to fly from venial sins as much as from mortal ones; and we should soon find that by the Divine assistance we are able to avoid venial sins as much as mortal ones. Ah! let us be well convinced that all the difficulty lies not in human weakness and frailty, which is remedied by the grace of God, but in our own will. If we do not will strongly, we cannot guard ourselves even from the most enormous mortal sins ; and if we will, we can also avoid even the smallest venial sin. I am referring, of course, to those of which we are fully conscious.

§ 7. *Shows that it is not too difficult for us to seek what is most pleasing to God in things that are themselves indifferent.*

A discreet master, a tender father, not only takes care not to impose on his servant or on his son anything too arduous and difficult, but does not even desire that his servants or his sons should undertake voluntarily to do for him things which are beyond their strength, and would end by becoming oppressive. Now certainly God is the most wise Master, the most tender Father, to us His servants, His children. Can we suppose that it can be His good pleasure to see us overburdened and afflicted in His service? What is most pleasing to God, in things indifferent in themselves, is to be found where our self-denial is proportionate to our strength in its measure, and the sacrifice endurable in itself. We wrong His ineffable goodness if we are afraid that, in order to please Him, we must make such an effort, such an exertion, that it would in some way exceed our powers, strengthened, of course (be it always understood), by the help of His grace. And here you must be careful not to be deceived by a false apprehension arising out of considerations of the greatness and sanctity of God. Considering that the greatness and sanctity of God are infinite, you might possibly imagine that only in the greatest and most holy things can God find His greatest pleasure, seeing that they only are, in some sort, worthy of Him. The supposition would be entirely false; for if God could find His greatest delight in such works only as are of themselves in some sort worthy of Him, He would never find what is most pleasing to Him in any works except in those of our Saviour Jesus Christ, which have infinite value and sanctity because they are the works of a Divine Person. Mere works of creatures, considered in themselves —be they those of the angels, or even of the most holy Virgin Mary herself—are but nothing, and therefore in no degree worthy of God, if you consider the proportions which they bear to the infinite excellency of His Divine Majesty. God finds His greatest delight, not in the grandeur and sanctity of works themselves, but in their conformity with His most Holy Will; and it certainly is not His Will that His creatures should perform the greatest and most holy works, but that they should perform those works which His love demands from them. And these are sometimes great, as when in martyrdom He requires the sacrifice of our lives; sometimes less, as when He commands us to conquer the desires of our perverse passions; sometimes very small, as when, according to circumstances, He asks from us some good aspiration or devout ejaculation.

For this reason we may really and truly endeavour to do what is most pleasing to God, even in things the slightest and easiest to be done.

And thus I have sufficiently proved to you that which I proposed to demonstrate—namely, that there is not too much difficulty in avoiding even venial sin, and in seeking to do that which is most pleasing to God, in things which are neither commanded nor prohibited. And so I have also proved that the attainment of Christian perfection is not too difficult a thing to do.

CHAPTER III.

THE OBJECTIONS USUALLY BROUGHT AGAINST THE FOREGOING DOCTRINES ARE SOLVED.

§ 1. *That it is not necessary to practise the evangelical counsels in order to attain Christian perfection.*

NOTWITHSTANDING what I have before said, perhaps, O devout soul, you may imagine that, in order to acquire Christian perfection or perfect sanctity, much more is demanded of us; and perhaps first of all you will ask me what account I have taken of the evangelical counsels, not having even once named them, whereas, in treating of perfection, they ought to come first. Do you, then, suppose the practice of the evangelical counsels to be necessary for the attainment of perfect sanctity? You are in error. First of all, as I told you, the angel of the schools, St. Thomas, only recognised as necessary for perfect sanctity the fulfilment of the Ten Commandments (see St. Thomas, 2—2, q. 184, a. 3); and such an authority ought to suffice for you. Nevertheless I wish to convince you by evident proofs. The evangelical counsels are three— Poverty, Obedience, and perfect Chastity. Now if it were true that the practice of these is necessary for the attainment of Christian perfection, it would be as much as to say that friars and nuns only could venture to aspire thereto. Married people would be excluded from it—all who do not live on alms, and do not renounce all that they possess, and all who do not give up absolutely their own will to the will of another. Therefore, since it is most true that God does not wish every one to practise the evangelical counsels, it would follow that He does not wish all to be saints, whereas the sacred Scriptures repeatedly assert that He does. The order of His providence requires that there should be continent people and married people; poor and rich; and He does not disapprove of some living free and independent, although He dearly loves that a man should submit himself to the will of another, and renounce his own will. Meanwhile He wills that all, according to their state, should become saints. Consequently it is a manifest error to assert that the practice of the evangelical counsels is necessary for the attainment of Christian sanctity.

§ 2. *Nor is it necessary to have extraordinary favours.*

You, however, among my readers who make a practice of reading the lives of the saints will possibly be surprised that I have reduced the attainment of sanctity to something so simple as avoiding deliberate venial sins and seeking that which is most pleasing to God in things indifferent, or, in other words, in things neither forbidden nor commanded, whilst we are accustomed to find sanctity usually united with extraordinary gifts and graces that are both surprising and deserving of admiration. You call to mind the gifts of ecstasy, of prophecy, of discerning spirits, of infused knowledge, of remarkable penance, &c., and possibly you are astonished that I appear to forget all this. Do you, then, believe that such extraordinary gifts and favours are requisite for the attainment of sanctity? You are again greatly in error. Such things are usually found in the lives of the saints, but these are not the means of forming saints; and in fact there are many souls gifted with none of these extraordinary favours who are yet more holy and deserve greater glory in Paradise than those who are enriched by them. For which reason St. Theresa assures us that in Heaven we shall find many exalted above those who during their lives on earth were privileged with extraordinary favours. Nay more, it must not be forgotten that sometimes even bad men have had some of these extraordinary gifts, like the impious Balaam, who had the gift of prophecy; and St. John of the Cross teaches (*Tratt. delle Spine*, coll. 2) that revelations, visions, ecstasies, the discerning and knowledge of spirits, and all the gifts which are called 'gratis datæ,' are not rarely coupled with mortal sin; whilst even the greatest saints have been entirely deprived of some of these gifts, like St. John the Baptist, who in all his life never performed a single miracle,— 'Joannes quidem signum fecit nullum' (Jo. x. 41). In like manner we nowhere read that the great archbishop, St. Charles Borromeo, was ever, during his most fervent prayers, rapt in ecstasy. Duly considering which things, all the masters of spirituality agree in teaching that we should not on any account venture to ask Almighty God to bestow upon us these extraordinary gifts—nay, that the desire for them would generally proceed from pride. Consequently, if you imagine that in order to become a saint you must be rapt in ecstasies, pass entire nights in prayer, wear a hair-shirt, take a little rest on the bare ground, pass whole days without eating, and do other marvellous things, you greatly err. To be a saint you must have the spirit of prayer; but it is not necessary that you should consume the whole night in prayer. Say the prayers that are prescribed for you by your spiritual director; and it is no matter if, instead of enjoying ecstasies and raptures, you are tormented by continued distractions and temptations. In order to be a saint you must have the spirit of mortification; but when you have performed the penances enjoined by your director and those that he may have permitted you to do, or any other little things which, by reason of their simplicity, may be done without permission — as, for instance, abstaining from some kind of fruit or other exquisite and delicate morsel, from looking at an object of curiosity, from listening to music, &c., which mortifications cannot have any evil consequences—you should rest satisfied, without pretending to anything more, persuaded that if you do other things out of your own caprice, instead of assisting yourself to grow in sanctity you will run the risk of becoming proud, and of endangering in more ways than one the health of both soul and body.

§ 3. *That God desires the greater part of mankind to be holy for their own sakes; and only a few for themselves and for others.*

But perhaps you will still find some difficulty

in persuading yourself of the truth of this doctrine, through not understanding why it is that God wishes you to be a saint without having any of those extraordinary gifts that illustrate the lives of the saints. If it be so, mark this well: God wishes us all to be holy, because He on His part desires that we should all inherit Paradise; and we know well that none but saints can enter Heaven. God wishes all to be holy; but some He wishes to be holy for their own sakes, some He wills to be holy for their own sake and for the sake of others also. I must explain myself. God wills that certain souls should acquire perfection, in order that they may have great glory in Heaven; and from these nothing is required in regard to others except the fulfilment of their duties and the good example which every one is bound to give to his neighbour. Therefore He wills that their holiness should shine with resplendent light before His Divine eyes, but He does not will that they should be equally resplendent in the eyes of the world—and observe that, among all the blessed souls, these are by far the greater number, although little known, because not distinguished by any admirable or extraordinary signs. How many there are (we who direct the consciences of men know, and praise

God for it)—how many there are, not merely among religious, but also among married people, among the rich, the poor, the learned, the ignorant, who find it easiest to live in great humility! Yes, you, O devout souls, that grieve at the sight of so many wicked people in this world outraging and blaspheming our good God, comfort yourselves by the thought that there are also very many good Christians in all conditions of life, who, seeking after perfection, serve our Lord faithfully, and who are very holy in His eyes, although not much so in the eyes of their fellow-men. Oh, how many you will see among the most exalted in Paradise who were very little distinguished upon earth! Be comforted, and try to be one of their number.

Nor should this surprise you, since they are most holy before God and merit the greatest glory in Heaven who have the most vivid faith, the firmest hope, the most burning charity; and faith, hope, and charity are interior virtues of the soul, which may exist in great perfection without making much external show. In fact St. Mary Magdalen de' Pazzi, in the ecstasy during which she saw the most surprising glory that St. Louis Gonzaga was enjoying in Paradise, did not ascribe it to his wonderful fasts, nor to his terrible disciplines, nor to

his prolonged vigils, but to his interior sanctity.
' O, what glory is bestowed on Louis, the son of
Ignatius !' thus she exclaimed. 'Never could I
have believed it if Thou, O my Jesus, hadst not
shown it to me. It seemed to me that there could
not be, so to say, such an excess of glory even in
Paradise as I see Louis now enjoying. I say that
Louis is a great saint. He is so glorified because
he laboured at the interior of his soul. Who can
ever express the value, the virtue of interior works?
There is no comparison between the interior and
the exterior.'

God also wills that other souls (and these are
few in number compared with those mentioned
above) should be most holy, not only as regards
themselves, but for the good of others also, so that
they may shine as admirable examples of sanctity,
and, attracting towards themselves the gaze of the
whole world, show manifestly forth to all men the
power and riches of His grace. On these souls He
bestows extraordinary gifts. They have the gift of
the sublimest prayer, so that they are able to pass
whole days and nights in communion with God,
and have ecstasies, being rapt out of themselves,
while their bodies, as if they were the lightest fea-
thers, are raised above the ground. They have

the gift of stupendous mortifications, in which they even pass the whole of Lent without food, bear up against the pain of terrible disciplines and the roughness of hair-shirts, hardly sleep at all, and take what little repose they give to their attenuated limbs on the bare ground, stretched on stones or blocks of wood. To these He makes known hidden things; He enables them to predict the future; He gives them power over diseases, and sometimes over death. Blessed be God, who has always continued to make His Church illustrious by these admirable examples of holiness! There were such in all centuries, as the history of past centuries teaches us; and without doubt there are some now, as may be proved by undeniable facts, which will equally enrich the annals of our times in future ages.

In these illustrious examples of sanctity we admire the majesty of God's omnipotence, the largeness of His mercy, the depth of His wisdom. We, seeing that these men, children of Adam, subject like ourselves to all human weaknesses and miseries, have yet arrived at such great things by the power of Divine grace,—we, who are spectators of these things, are encouraged in all the difficulties which this unhappy life on earth brings upon us, and we gain confidence from their example, trusting that we shall be able to overcome all that opposes our progress on the road to heaven. And if we do anything that is good, we are forced to humble ourselves profoundly before them, for our good works appear as nothing by comparison with theirs. At all events we cannot flatter ourselves that God places us among their number. Listen to St. Francis of Sales (Serm. 6th, for Ash-Wednesday): 'In this world some are called to lead a life entirely angelic and celestial, which we should reverently admire, not that we should copy their actions, but that we may bless God for the graces He bestowed on them.' And then he cites the cases of St. Paul the Hermit and St. Simon Stylites, saying 'that they were moved by a special inspiration from God, so that they were enabled to become a spectacle and prodigy of holiness, to be admired but not imitated.'

§ 4. *That we cannot aspire to be chosen by God as sublime examples of holiness.*

We have no reason to presume that God should bestow on us the extraordinary favours indicated in the foregoing paragraph, since they are not necessary for our sanctification, and perhaps, according to the adorable dispositions of His providence, they are not in any way destined for us. Would it not be real pride not to content ourselves with that holiness which would make us good and holy in the eyes of His Divine Majesty, but to desire furthermore those admirable gifts and favours which would make us appear good and holy before the world? Mark well that the desire to be very holy before God is the offspring of holy humility, but the desire to appear so before men is the daughter of accursed pride.

And, in fact, do you imagine that the great saints chosen by God as luminaries in His Church, and consequently enriched with many extraordinary favours and admirable graces, desired to possess these gifts and favours? Oh, how much you are deceived if you imagine this to be the case! Let these two examples suffice for all the others that might be adduced.

§ 5. *Gives the example of saints who through humility regretted having extraordinary gifts.*

St. Mary Magdalen de' Pazzi was endowed by God with very many singular graces, and amongst others that of enduring extraordinary penances and mortifications in the way of eating, by which she

was distinguished from all the other nuns her companions. But do you think that she asked Almighty God to give her such favours? On the contrary, she grieved very much at being obliged to make herself so singular, desired that she might be allowed to eat the food of the community, and only surrendered herself to this extraordinary life when God Himself made known to her, in an ecstasy, His express will that she should make these fasts, and told her that, if she refused to obey, He would withdraw the light of His Divine eyes from her,—
'Si hoc non facies retraham abs te oculos meos.'

St. Joseph of Cupertino was, in like manner, among the number of those saints who received from God the most extraordinary graces and favours. He prophesied things to come, knew the depths of men's hearts, enjoyed the sweetest ecstasies and stupendous raptures, gave forth from his most chaste body a wonderful odour, and wrought miraculous cures, so that every one venerated him as a great saint; and although he was an humble friar, princes esteemed it a great advantage to be able to do him honour. But perhaps St. Joseph had desired these wonderful gifts? perhaps he wished them to be continued? On the contrary, he besought the Lord most fervently that He would deign to de-

D

prive him of these gifts, desiring to live the ordinary life of the community, and not be distinguished from any one. Now could these souls, elevated as they were to so high a degree of sanctity—could they have felt sorry at being favoured by God with such graces, if they had believed such graces to be in the smallest degree requisite in order to love God perfectly? On the contrary, they would have been most delighted, and they would have continually besought God to bestow on them new and still more wonderful favours, that they might continually grow, as it was their sole desire to do, in His holy love and in Christian perfection. Hearken to St. Theresa (*Mansions*): 'Those who receive many supernatural graces and favours do not merit thereby a greater degree of glory; nay, they are under a greater obligation to serve God.'

§ 6. *Conclusion of the answer to objections.*

You see, then, that you are wrong in supposing that I desire to make you acquire holiness by any other means than those used by the saints.

Rest assured that the saints did not arrive at so high a degree of perfection before God by means of extraordinary gifts and marvellous favours, but by the exercise of Christian virtues, with perfect conformity to the Divine Will. Certainly by means of these extraordinary and marvellous gifts they also reached a high degree of perfection in the opinion of men; but this was in no way necessary for Christian perfection. Show me that God wills you to be among the number of these few, that He chooses you to be lights in the world, and consequently wills you to appear great in the eyes of men, and then I will say to you that you must tread the same path that the saints of whom we read have trodden. If, on the other hand, you are among the greater number of those others who are called by God to that sanctity which is beautiful in His sight alone, and not to be manifested to the world in all its brightness until the last day, be content to travel along the ordinary road, and do not pretend to higher things, lest you end by being proud instead of holy. If a hen tried to fly above the clouds like the eagle, would you not laugh at her presumption? She must have the wings of the eagle in order to fly like him.

Let us conclude, then, that in order to be saints, and even great saints, before God, nothing extraordinary is required of us; and that consequently, on this head, the way of perfection is made much easier.

§ 7. *That human weakness does not render the attainment of Christian perfection too difficult.*

Although extraordinary and marvellous things are not required for the attainment of Christian perfection, and it suffices that we should abstain from all sins of which we are fully aware, whether grave or light ones, and seek that which is most pleasing to God in things indifferent,—after all this, you will tell me that there still remains a most grave difficulty in human weakness and frailty, which renders a full and exact obedience to the Divine laws beyond measure difficult. Do not be afraid—take courage! Even this third difficulty is one more apparent than real. And pray tell me, are you speaking of human weakness and frailty abandoned to itself, or are you speaking of it as strengthened and confirmed by the omnipotent aid of Divine grace? If you are speaking of human weakness and frailty abandoned to its own resources alone, you are certainly right; nay more, I confess to you my firm belief that it would not only be very difficult, but wholly impossible, to fulfil all the precepts of the laws of God. But if, instead of this, you are speaking of human weakness and frailty strengthened and confirmed by the omnipotence of the grace of God, you are certainly wrong, very wrong, and err greatly in supposing that the fulfilment of all the Divine laws would be too difficult for us. It would be difficult, nay impossible, for a child to lift a great weight from the ground, but with the help of a strong man he can do so easily. And is it not of faith that the power of the grace of God assists our weakness, strengthens our frailty, so that we are enabled to fulfil all the Divine commands? Hearken to the most consoling doctrine of the holy Council of Trent : 'God does not command what is impossible; but when He commands He warns you to do what you can, and to ask for assistance in those things which you are unable to do. Meanwhile He assists you, in order that you may be able to do them. His commands are not heavy, His yoke is sweet, His burden light.' Oh, most consoling doctrine! and all the more consoling because it is the doctrine of the Holy Spirit—infallible doctrine! Is it not likewise of faith that God does not permit us to be tempted by our enemies beyond what our strength, assisted by His grace, can enable us to bear? Hearken to those other most consoling and infallible words dictated by the Holy Ghost, who thus assures us, through the mouth of St. Paul, 'that God is faithful, who will not suffer you to be tempted above that which you are able, but will make also with temptation issue, that you may be able to bear it' (1 Cor. x. 13). Which means this: God has promised to assist our weakness, and to restrain the wrath and fury of our enemies, so that they will not be able to overcome us in their assaults; nay, He therefore favours us with as much grace as will enable us to come out of the strongest temptation stronger than before, as a soldier, coming victorious from a battle, acquires for subsequent battles greater courage (see Corn. à Lap.). St. Theresa also says, 'It does not disturb me to see a soul in the midst of very great temptations; for if it have the love and fear of God, it will come out of them with much gain' (*Conc. dell' Am. di Diò sulla Cant.*). What is meant, then, when it is said that we are weak—that we are frail? It means that if the grace of God were to abandon us, the full observance of the laws of God would be quite impossible for us; but it does not mean that this full obedience would be too difficult when assisted, as we are, by heavenly grace. Observe also that when Almighty God wills to bestow on any soul a great degree of eminence in any given virtue, ordinarily speaking He permits that soul to undergo very strong temptations against that particular virtue. He dealt so with St. Paul—'nam virtus in infirmitate perficitur,' —'for power is made perfect in infirmity'. For this reason, if you have strong temptations against faith, it means that God wills to bestow upon you a very vivid faith. If against chastity, it means that God wills to enrich you with very perfect chastity. This is a thing that you ought to mark well and observe attentively, because it is just the reason why many people despair of being able to arrive at Christian perfection. They base their calculations upon their own strength, and not upon the strength of the grace of God. Let us understand fully this great truth; for by ourselves we are nothing, and we are good for nothing; but by the grace of God we are somewhat, and become capable of all things.

§ 8. *That the truly humble should not lose confidence on account of their own weakness.*

If we were truly humble we should never be terrified by any difficulty we might encounter in the service of God; for if we were truly humble we should be inwardly persuaded that we are not only able to do very little, but able to do nothing at all. And, in fact, what can man, left to himself, accomplish? Absolutely nothing in the natural order as in the supernatural. Without the concurrence of Almighty God in the natural order we could not move an arm; without His concurrence in the supernatural order we could not even invoke the name of Jesus. Meanwhile, were we fully persuaded of this truth, great difficulties would no longer alarm us. Does this seem to you a paradox? Yet it is the simple truth. A man who is truly convinced that he has in himself no power to do anything good of any kind recognises the fact that all power to do what is right must come from God; and therefore he looks to God for it. So he continually seeks the assistance of God, and expects it as well in little things as in the greater and more important undertakings which he may have on hand. Meantime he clearly sees that all things are great or little only in our own eyes; that all things are as nothing before God, since all are equally easy to Him; that it is the same thing for Almighty God to make a leaf fall from a tree or to create a world. Therefore, in no way trusting to himself, but placing all his confidence in God, he considers himself able to do all things, and is terrified at nothing in the service of his Divine Master. The mischief is, that we accustom ourselves to draw distinctions between one thing and another, calling some things small and others great. Through not keeping in mind our absolute incapacity to do anything rightly, we flatter ourselves that we can succeed in the former; and then, not reflecting on the power of the Divine assistance, by virtue of which we are able to do all things, we despair of being able to accomplish the latter. Ah! let us be persuaded that we must seek continually from God, and expect from Him, all power, whether for little things or great ones. Then the consideration of our own weakness can never deprive us of courage, and our confidence will be invincible. And, in truth, was it not the saints who undertook and brought to a good termination the greatest, the most difficult works, and undertook them also without any of the means which ordinarily would have been considered indispensable? Were they overbold? were they imprudent? Assuredly not; they knew that God required of them these works for His service, and this knowledge was sufficient for them. They knew that they were about to work with God, to whom nothing is impossible, and they were confident that they should be equally successful in great and in little things.

St. Cyprian and St. Augustine before their conversion, considering only their own frailty, did not believe it possible for them to succeed in abstaining even from mortal sin. They thought that it was almost impossible to observe the laws of God. But when they were converted they found in practice that, through the Divine grace, they succeeded in abstaining not only from mortal sin, but from venial sin also. Hence they had positive proof that by His aid it is not difficult to become a saint, even a great saint. Mark what St. Paul says: 'I can do all things through God, who strengthens me.' He was not content with saying, 'I can do *some* things,' but 'all things.' He, then, would never have thought of keeping himself only from mortal sins just to obtain salvation. Nay, he thought it by far the best to be able to abstain from venial sins also, and thereby hope to attain the very high glory that those have in Heaven who on earth aspire to arrive at perfect sanctity.

§ 9. *That bad natural dispositions cannot make it too difficult to acquire Christian perfection.*

Similar to that of human frailty is the impediment of our evil nature, by which so many excuse themselves from endeavouring to become saints;

OBJECTIONS SOLVED. 43

and perhaps you who read this find in yourselves a great obstacle, very difficult to surmount. Well, let us hear what your natural defects are. Perhaps you have a choleric nature, that resents the smallest contradiction and annoyance? At some rudeness or some offence you feel your blood almost changed into fire? This being the case, the exercise of gentleness and humility appears to you too difficult a thing, though they are virtues fundamentally necessary for Christian perfection. You must observe, by the bye, that, as St. Thomas says, all wrath is not bad; and there is a just anger. 'Do not imagine,' says the holy doctor, 'that anger is a passion which is to be compared with pride, or envy, or other such things as of themselves are always evil and abominable.' Anger, he goes on to say, is a passion necessary to man, as St. John Chrysostom warns us. 'Anger is the instrument of virtue,' as St. Gregory the Great adds (in 5th book of *Moral.* c. liii.). The evil of anger consists in being angry without sufficient cause, or in being angry beyond measure. Whoever is angry in a just cause, and with moderation, acts well, not ill. If any one should feel a scruple about the disturbance and agitation which, by a necessary and natural consequence, is caused by anger in our minds, since it is impossible to be angry and yet preserve unalterably our internal peace, St. Thomas reminds us that when anger is just, and regulated by reason, the disturbance and agitation caused by it are not in any way sinful. Hence he teaches us that well-regulated anger is not opposed to the virtue of gentleness, and that this passion (of course most perfectly kept in its proper order) is likewise to be found in the Divine Lamb, our Lord Jesus Christ (p. iii. q. 15, a. 9).* Which most sound doctrine of the angelic doctor I have wished thus to expound to its full extent, because there are ascetic books which, through excessive scrupulosity lest any offence against gentleness be committed, would not permit us ever to be angry, forgetting that our Lord Christ Himself was angry several times, particularly against the Pharisees, on whom (it is written) He looked with anger,—'circumspiciens eos cum irâ' (St. Mark iii. 5). Hence if it were true that to be angry is always an imperfection, it would be an imperfection taught us by our Divine Master Himself. Anger is a passion which may be compared with love; and love is not evil unless it be inordinate. Nor is the argument of theirs worth anything which they put forth to justify their

* See Note 1.

doctrine, that although in the abstract there may be a just anger, yet in practice the risk of falling into excess or defect is so great that it is better never to be angry at all, even justly, than to run the risk of being angry in a wrong way. Reasoning of this kind would drive one to the conclusion that in this world it is better to do nothing at all than to do something. Indeed where should we be able to find anything in which we could not commit faults—nay, in which we do not commit them often? I repeat that anger is a passion, like love, which when it is just and moderate is good, and when it is distorted and immoderate is evil. Now in love, as well as in anger, we can commit, and do commit, faults; but would it be a right doctrine to teach that people ought to suppress every sentiment of love, however good, for fear of the defects which may and do usually accompany it? Parents may err, and sometimes do so, from over-love of their children; husband and wife, in their mutual love, do likewise. Should we in consequence teach that parents ought to suppress every sentiment of affection for their children, and that husbands and wives should love each other no longer? On the contrary, we content ourselves with telling them to guard themselves against those defects into which from excess of love they may, and do, so easily fall; and at the same time we approve and commend their love, as being proper and indeed their duty.

We must, then, distinguish bad anger from good. Evil anger is that which is awakened in us when inordinate self-love is wounded, or when there is no just cause for being angry, or when, though there is a just cause, it passes the limits of due moderation. Just anger is that which, without overpassing the boundaries of due moderation, is excited in our hearts at seeing offences committed against Almighty God, duty transgressed, virtue trodden down. Thus superiors must often be angry, in order to correct the excesses of those under their authority; persons solicited to sin must be angry with those who assail their honour; every soul that loves God must feel embittered by the wickednesses of sinners. Having elucidated this point, which to some people is rather obscure, we will return to our subject.

You have, perhaps, a very irascible nature? This means that, when there is anything to be angry at, you easily become angry. In the Old Testament we have many examples of holy people who were quick-tempered when there was just cause for anger. And indeed were not Noe and Moses ready to be angry, although Moses was 'vir mitissimus super omnes homines qui morabantur in terra' (Num. xii. 3),—'a man exceeding meek above all men that dwelt upon earth'? and David, Elias, Eliseus, and so many others? We have an infinite number of examples of holy anger among the most celebrated saints of the Church. They knew when to be angry with the persecutors who blasphemed Christ and endeavoured to force them to do things unworthy of Christians. And were they not easily indignant with heretics? And was not their anger quick and strong against bad Christians, especially so when their evil doings tended to the corruption of morals? How much severity of holy anger do we sometimes find in the writings of St. John Chrysostom, St. Jerome, and even the usually gentle and sweet St. Bernard!

'But they,' you will reply, 'were angry without sinning.' This is just what you must be, by the grace of the Lord. When you are surprised by anger on account of some misfortune, some injury, some wrong or affront, suppress it as soon as you discover it. You should not be angry about these things, which God permits for your good, to keep you detached from the world, confident in Him alone, and above all things humble. I say 'as soon as you are aware of it,' because so long as it is unintentional, however bad it may be, it is nevertheless not a sin. Then when it comes on you because you see offences offered to God, duties transgressed; virtue vilified, and you feel still more angry because these things have been done by those who are placed under your authority, be content to bridle it, that it may not in an unruly manner overpass the limits of what is just and right; but do not imagine that you are called upon to stifle it altogether, as if it were only a fire made to burn and destroy. A just anger is a fire that is necessary to give warmth and life to our zeal for the glory of God and the salvation of our neighbour; nay, it is not distinguishable from this holy zeal, and it is called so by St. Thomas. Therefore if you have an irascible nature bridle it according to the teaching of reason and of faith, but console yourself with the reflection that you are the more naturally disposed to the more lively and powerful operations of the holy love of God. In the mean while do not imagine that you ought to deface this your natural disposition, and transform it into its opposite. Such an undoing, such a complete alteration, you ought not even to ask from God. Ask Him rather for grace to make good use of your natural disposition, taking care that you are never angry without just cause, and that even your just anger never overpasses the limits of your duty. You may then rest assured that your natural disposition, however irascible it may be, will coöperate excellently well in bringing about your sanctification. When one reads of such and such a saint having changed his fiery nature into one of gentleness, this expression only means that by the virtue of gentleness he has moderated the excesses of irascibility; and this you also should do. Should you reply: 'I shall commit faults,' I answer you, that faults you will commit in some way, whatever your natural disposition may be. Try to prevent these faults from being conscious and deliberate ones, and with this rest satisfied, for this satisfies Almighty God. Meanwhile your carefulness and your efforts to moderate that anger, which unbridled would lead to excess, will crown you in Paradise with an amount of merit and glory of which you have no conception. An expert horseman has little credit for riding a quiet horse, but much for managing a fiery one, that besides will get over more ground in less time.

It may be that it is your nature to err by excess of coldness. Then you should try to rouse yourself as much as possible, so that a reprehensible indolence, a false gentleness, should not cause you to fail in your duty, and especially so if there are those placed under you whom you ought to watch over and correct. It is too true indeed that there are some people who, under the disguise of an ill-understood meekness and contemptible patience, allow disorders to take their course uninterruptedly, and permit offences against God, when they could prevent them; but you, by gaining Divine grace, which is a fire that warms the cold heart, will watch carefully over your duties, and not fall into those faults; whilst, on the other hand, you will have the consolation of finding yourself the more disposed to the exercise of true gentleness and patience, which are virtues necessary for the attainment of Christian perfection.

But perhaps your natural disposition is too tender, too sensitive, so that your heart is very easily enkindled with an inordinate love for creatures, and a glance, a word, awakens in you the fire of a great passion; whence you judge that you cannot reasonably hope ever to attain that purity of heart which cannot be dissevered from Christian perfection. If it be true that your heart is extraordinarily tender and sensitive to all suggestions of that passion which is the most to be feared in this miserable world, there is no doubt that you ought most cautiously to keep guard over it, defend it, fortify it, so that it should receive none of those wounds which, alas, are so often almost incurable.

You should avoid unnecessary converse with those of the opposite sex, keep a cautious watch over your eyes, be on your guard against all dangerous pastimes and dangerous books,—do in fact what every good Christian should do, though he be not as sensitive as yourself. Perhaps you fancy that less sensitive people need less caution than yourself? But these, when they feel persuaded, as they sometimes do, that they have nothing to fear, carelessly tread a path which is for us all but too muddy and slippery, and hence have to lament more frequent falls. If you retain in your heart a holy fear of God, the sensitiveness which to you appears overmastering and extremely perilous will prove to be a most useful safeguard, almost a defence and security, because it will always keep you watchful and prudent, ever diffident of yourself, ever intent on imploring the Divine assistance in all things. On this, and not on coldness and natural insensibility, is based the certain hope of freedom from danger of sinning; and hence it arises that the purest hearted are most frequently found among the most sensitive persons—a fact that we who are directors of souls observe every day.

Meanwhile it is wise to condescend to people's natural dispositions, except in what is vicious or not quite right; therefore give vent to the sensibility of your soul by the exercise of a holy fraternal charity for the souls as well as the bodies of others, showing yourself to be most sensitive to the disease of the soul—that is, to sin—and tender towards the temporal wants of your brothers in Christ, according to the rules of the holy Gospel. Give vent also to your tenderness in the remembrance of our Lord's bitter Passion, in a loving reception of Him in the most Holy Communion, in devout visits to His tabernacle, in devotion to Mary. May not a sensitive and tender heart thus become a saintly heart?

But if, on the contrary, you are naturally hard and insensible, and therefore little fitted for the tender emotions of love and devotion, do not imagine that by reason of this you cannot become holy. Our Lord does not require from you sensitiveness and tender emotions, but strong love —the solid love of the will—that is, as I have told you before, the uniformity of our will with His Will; and this uniformity may be most perfect without being accompanied by any sensibility or tenderness. Moreover, if it should be His Will to grant you all this, it is not necessary that your disposition should be one naturally inclined to such emotions. A heart that is naturally as hard and insensible as a stone can, at the loving visit of His grace, be dissolved into the most tender emotions of love, as wax melts before the fire. If, however, God does not so favour you, but leaves you in your state of cold insensibility, do not be afraid on that account. By serving Him perseveringly without that sense of sweetness, without those rewards, and therefore without any sensible satisfaction in so doing, you will have the more merit, and God the greater glory.

But let us conclude this subject of the natural disposition. The various natures of all the sons and daughters of Adam are, each of them, in one way or another, defective and inclined to evil. The grace of God is sufficient to correct and amend every natural disposition, even the worst. Confide in Him, watch over yourself, and, whatever natural disposition you may happen to have, you will become holy.

§ 10. *Shows that it is not too difficult for us to gain the necessary power of self-denial.*

And now methinks I hear you bring forward

another argument, which perhaps you think more grave than the preceding. You will tell me that, in enumerating the things which are required in order to progress towards Christian perfection, I have been silent about that which is the foundation of all, namely, self-denial, the necessity of which is so clearly taught in the Gospels, and recommended with so much fervour by all masters in spirituality. 'Can I become holy,' you will say, 'without denying myself—that is, without renouncing my inclinations and my desires? But if I must give up all my inclinations and all my desires, shall I not find the gravest difficulty in such self-denial?' Do you imagine, then, that I would exclude the denial of oneself from the means necessary for acquiring Christian perfection? By the mere suspicion you do me a great wrong. I too know and believe that self-denial is necessary for the acquirement of Christian perfection—nay, I say more. I know and believe that self-denial is indispensable to prevent us from falling into mortal sin, and to keep us simply in a state of grace. I know and believe that without this self-denial no one can be a good disciple of Christ, who says: 'If any man will follow Me, let him deny himself.' But, on the other hand, you must well understand in what this necessary self-denial consists. It consists in contradicting every inclination which is in any way inordinate. Therefore it consists, first of all, in renouncing those inclinations that would lead us into mortal sin, such as the inclination to serious revenge, inclinations to immorality, &c.; secondly, in resisting those that would lead to venial sin, such as officious lying, small thefts, and the rest, and also those that would hinder us from doing what we know to be most pleasing to God, such as the inclination not to yield to another some small right which in strict justice we might retain, and which, notwithstanding, it is better to yield for the sake of fraternal charity. In these things consists the self-denial necessary for the acquirement of Christian perfection.

You say that 'you ought to oppose all your inclinations and all your wishes;' but you are utterly wrong. As a matter of fact, you have an inclination to eat, and you must eat; you have an inclination to sleep, and you must sleep; you have an inclination to take a suitable recreation after long and serious occupations, and it is necessary you should take it. You are only required to oppose those desires and inclinations which are in some way inordinate, like those which I pointed out. Now since I have taught you that you should avoid not only mortal sin, but venial sins also, and that in things neither commanded nor forbidden you should seek to conform yourself to those which are most pleasing to God, you will see, if you consider well what I have said, that I have clearly taught you the necessity of self-denial; and since I have demonstrated to you that these three things are not too difficult for you to accomplish, I have necessarily demonstrated to you also that to deny ourselves is not too great a difficulty for us. And mark well. All the perfection of self-denial practised by saints consists in those three things; because even those saints whose mortifications were most conspicuous did not oppose their inclinations and wishes except where it was advisable to do so for the avoidance of sin, or for the exercise of those acts of mortification which they knew were pleasing to God, according to what He required from them through ordinary or extraordinary inspirations regulated by the advice of their spiritual directors.

The word 'self-denial,' understood in its rigidly material signification, terrifies many, because they imagine it to mean a continual thwarting of oneself without any discretion; and so people come to the conclusion that they would not be able to persevere —at least for any length of time—in practising it. But if we understand it in its true signification, according to the spirit of the Gospel which taught it, no one could be dismayed or discouraged, because it means neither more nor less than the observance of the Divine law, which is an easy yoke and a light burden. If, then, you should meet with books that speak of self-denial in a different sense, and require more than that which I have inculcated, you may conclude either that they are inexact, or that they are speaking emphatically, and therefore must in consequence be interpreted with due discretion. I am not at all afraid of being mistaken, for these opinions of mine are conformable to the doctrine of St. Thomas and of all theologians.

§ 11. *Nor is it too difficult to seek, in all things, what is most pleasing to God.*

But possibly you imagine that the greatest difficulty of all is having to seek in all things that which is most pleasing to God. It appears to you that the burden of this constant attention must keep you in perpetual solicitude and distress. 'I must apply myself,' you will say, perhaps, 'to study in all things that which shall please God the most; and this search will raise in me continual doubt, a perpetual uncertainty, which will destroy my peace.' But here again there is a great mistake. It is not at all required of us that we should try to find out what is most pleasing to God in everything whatsoever; as, for instance, 'would it please God most that I should go now to hear Mass or to hear a sermon? that I should say the Rosary or recite the Office for the Dead? that I should breakfast this morning or fast? that I should give such an alms to the poor or to the Church?' I should take good care not to advise such researches as these for finding out what is most pleasing to God. Generally speaking, it would be nothing else but driving souls into a perpetual state of anguish and confusion. Let those souls that are given to such minutiæ attend to the maxims of St. Francis of Sales : 'It is not usual to weigh small coin, but only money of greater value. Buying and selling would be too tiresome, and would take up too much time, if we were obliged to weigh the farthings, the pence, and other small money. In like manner, we ought not to weigh all our minute actions, to try whether one is worth more than another'

(*Treatise on the Love of God*). Simplicity and freedom of soul is necessary in all things. Perfection requires us to do those things which we clearly know to be most agreeable to God; for, according to the docrine of St. Thomas, we cannot be bound to fulfil the Divine Will except so far as it is manifested to us (i. 2, q. 19, a. 10 ad 3); and in this there can be neither distress nor confusion. For example, I have leisure to hear holy Mass every day. Well, then, although we are not commanded to hear Mass on weekdays, I clearly see that to hear Mass would be more pleasing to God than to neglect doing so. I have time to frequent the most Blessed Sacrament, as my confessor—although he does not order it—exhorts me to do. Therefore I clearly see that I should do what is more pleasing to God by frequenting the Blessed Sacrament than by abstaining from doing so. In some particular instance I might maintain that a person who had done me a wrong ought to bow to me first; nevertheless I see that, for the sake of holy charity, it would be better that I should first bow to him. What possible anxiety, what distress or confusion can it give us to know that in such things we should do what is most pleasing to God? Nothing is wanted but an ardent love of God, and then all is accomplished.

Does not a son who loves his father do his best to satisfy him? Does not a daughter try to do likewise who tenderly loves her mother? Does not a servant do so if he is very fond of his master? Do you suppose that this son, this daughter, this servant, are troubled and disturbed in what they do? Quite the contrary. What is done for love and lovingly is done with freedom and cheerfulness. Try to be a little more earnest in the love of God, and then you will see that, instead of finding trouble and anxiety in endeavouring to do that which is most pleasing to Him, you will find great peace and much sweet satisfaction. Indeed you must see that this follows naturally; for since you have made the resolution never to displease God willingly—not even by committing venial sin—fulfilling exactly His most Holy Will in whatever He commands you to do, be it small or great, you will, as a natural consequence, find yourself imperceptibly carried on to do, even in things that are indifferent, that which is most pleasing to Him, all that you know to be most agreeable to His most Holy Will. And remember also that the same Divine love will enlighten you to know the good pleasure of God in many things that would be obscure to others; for Divine love is a fire which inflames us to act with quickness and fervour; and is also a light to illuminate us, so that we can see clearly what we ought to do.

All these reasons, however, will be useless, and you will never understand the truth of what I am telling to you, unless you put it to the proof. The words of St. Francis of Assisi are much to the point here : 'Tantum scit homo quantum operatur' (Nat. Alex. t. ix. a. 7, ex Phil.) ; which means, you have no true knowledge of what you have not worked out yourself. If you will do what I tell you, you will then understand that it can be done, that it is right to do it, and that it is done easily. Let me conclude in the words of St. Theresa : 'The soul that truly loves God, perceiving and knowing that one thing is of greater perfection than another, and more acceptable to God,—such a soul, by reason of the satisfaction it feels in pleasing God, carries out the same without difficulty ; the Divine Majesty assisting and giving courage and vigour to its weakness.'

§ 12. *Neither can the perils of the world nor family cares, &c., hinder our sanctification.*

But if you happen to be one of those too timorous and too diffident souls, you might again object to me : ' How can I become holy in the state of life in which I am placed ? In the midst of the world, surrounded with perils, oppressed with cares for my family, obliged to work hard, to buy and sell, how can I give my mind to the attainment of Christian perfection?' Hear what St. Alphonsus says in his *Practice of the Love of Jesus Christ* (g. viii. § 10): 'The monk should become holy as a monk, the layman as a layman, the priest as a priest, the married man in a state of marriage, the soldier while following his calling.' And certainly, since God desires that all should become saints, He will give to all the necessary graces, that they may become holy in whatever state or condition of life they may be placed. Do not these various states of life exist in this world by the disposition of God's providence? and can we suppose Him to have ordained that there shall be certain states of life in which it is impossible to become holy, while at the same time He requires holiness from all? Fear not; only have the will, and in spite of all your family cares and business, yes, in the midst of this world's inevitable perils, you will attain Christian perfection, according to your state. I have already said that God, according to our needs, gives us His grace; and so true is it that each one, according to his state, may become holy, that St. Francis of Sales disapproves of those who, finding themselves employed in one condition of life, nourish the desire to enter upon another. Listen to his words: 'I do not approve of those persons who, being attached to any given employment or vocation, persist in desiring any other kind of life not conformable to their office or occupation.' In confirmation of this truth, we have before us the fact that among the saints who are venerated on our altars there are some of every condition and every state of life.

§ 13. *Shows that business and laborious work, family cares, and all the other occupations consequent on our condition in life, may be made to assist us greatly in the attainment of Christian perfection.*

I am not content, however, with proving to you that the occupations belonging to your state of life are not impediments that must oblige you to abandon the hope of acquiring Christian perfection ; I wish to prove to you besides that they can greatly assist you in its attainment. And, as a matter of fact, are the employments belonging to each state of life bad in themselves? Certainly not. Of course I am not supposing that you are engaged in sinful trades. Your occupations are in themselves indifferent, either business or study or manual labour ; or perhaps you live on your income, and employ yourself in superintending the proper cultivation of your estates and the proper regulation of your rents, &c. These occupations are not in themselves holy; but neither are they bad. Well, then, do you not yet understand that occupations and labours indifferent in themselves, when they are undertaken and carried on in and for the love of God, directed and offered up for His glory, become holy and meritorious? You fancy that you lose time on the way to Paradise by attending to your trade and keeping your accounts, by your daily labour or by regulating your family affairs. Certainly you may lose time in these and similar occupations, if you undertake them merely to gain human ends, without having any regard to the glory of God. But if, on the contrary, all your occupations are offered up to God from time to time (it will be the best way to offer them daily), with the intention of doing all things for His glory, do they not at once become sanctified by that good intention, and most useful as a means to increase your love of God, and make you more deserving of Paradise? In this way will they not aid you in your progress towards Christian perfection? One day St. Philip Neri saw some day-labourers working very hard and perspiring much with the exertions of their heavy labour; and he asked them, 'Why are you working so hard?'

'Ah, father,' they answered, 'to gain our bread.'

'No, dear children,' replied the saint; 'do not say to gain your bread only, but to gain your bread and to win Paradise also.'

You see, then, that all your works, and all the employments of your condition in life, may be made to help you most exceedingly for the good of your souls, for your growth in the love of God, and for your progress in Christian perfection. O, if we would but do all for the love of God! if we would but direct all our actions to His glory! Then even those things which in themselves are, so to speak, but mud and stones, would be transformed into gold, into jewels of eternal life.

§ 14. *That albeit we are unworthy, we ought to hope for the grace of sanctity.*

Possibly the demon will say, 'You think, then, that you have a right to expect from God so great a grace as that of becoming a saint? Ought you not rather to be contented with the lowest place in Paradise?'

Nonsense! Hear St. Augustine: 'Ab Omnipotente petitis aliquid? magnum petite.' If you ask anything of the Omnipotent God, ask something great. What? Does it cost God more to give you a great grace than a small one? And (let me repeat again and again) if God desires that you should become holy, will it displease Him to bestow on you the necessary graces? Listen, then, to St. Theresa in her *Path of Perfection:* 'Does it cost us anything, or prejudice our cause, to ask for much when we are asking it from the Omnipotent God? It would be a shame to us were we to ask a great and most liberal emperor for a farthing.' Why, then, would you wish to be contented with the lowest place in Paradise? The soul that in Paradise will have the lowest place is the soul which will have done the least for the glory of God on earth, and consequently will give Him the least glory in heaven. Why, then, since you have the power of giving greater glory to God in time and in eternity, do you wish to be contented with giving Him less? As if Almighty God did not deserve that you should do what you can for Him. The soul that shall have the lowest place in Heaven will be fully satisfied with having gained that place, because in heaven there is no such thing as disappointment; but while we are in this world we ought not to rest satisfied with striving merely to gain the lowest place. Rather should we desire to gain a very high one by aiming at Christian perfection, in order to give our God the greater glory in time and in eternity.

'You indeed do not deserve the grace of Christian perfection. And what do you think about the many sins of your past life? and your ingratitude, and your unfaithfulness?' All this the demon may insist on; and indeed I also am fully persuaded that you do not deserve this grace. But what of that? Are you only to expect from our Lord what you deserve to have? Is this to be our hope—that God will treat us according to our own merits? God keep us from a hope of this kind! If God were to treat us as we deserve, should we not be all lost? We ought to hope after the manner in which we ought to pray. Tell me now, O devout soul, would you think of saying such a prayer as this: 'O Lord, treat me according to my deserts?' Would you not be afraid of saying such a prayer as this? In fact it would not be a prayer at all, but a horrible imprecation uttered against ourselves. To pray to God that He would treat us according to our deserts is equivalent to praying that He would abandon us to our own wickedness, and precipitate us into the infernal abyss; for nothing less do we of our own selves deserve. How, then, could we hope that God would treat us in this manner? Such a hope would not be hope, but despair. Even the greatest saints in paradise, if they had been dealt with according to their own merits—what would have become of them? where would they be? God treated them according to the infinite merits of Jesus Christ, who redeemed them by His Precious Blood; and in this way they have come to be great saints in heaven. We in like manner ought to hope, and steadfastly to hope, that He will deign to treat us also according to these infinite merits, which are greater than the magnitude of our sins—greater than all our ingratitude and unfaithfulness. What, then, do they mean who say that on account of your many sins and the rest you do not deserve to receive the grace of becoming holy? Simply this, Be truly penitent for your many sins, your ingratitude, and your unfaithfulness, keeping strict watch over yourself for the future; and then these sins and imperfections will not hinder Almighty God from granting you the grace of the sanctity you desire, which was merited for you by the infinite merits of His Incarnate Son, who died for you on the cross. As a matter of fact, how many great saints, now venerated on our altars, were at first great sinners? What the mercy and grace of God has accomplished in them can He not accomplish in you? Well, then, we come to this conclusion—that for no one—absolutely for no one—is the attainment of Christian perfection too difficult; such perfection, as we have already said, consisting in the perfect union of our wills with the Will of God.

CHAPTER IV.

ON THE BEAUTY AND UTILITY OF CHRISTIAN PERFECTION.

§ 1. *The beauty of Christian perfection.*

WHEN any given object has the double gift of beauty and usefulness, it attracts people's hearts towards it with a sweet violence, forces them to love it, and makes them desire to possess it. Now since I desire that you should so become enamoured of Christian perfection that you may seek with great diligence to arrive at the happy possession of it, I would bring before your eyes some portion at least of its celestial beauty, and afterwards a few reasons why it is so incomparably useful.

And to begin with the first of these gifts. How beautiful is that holiness which consists in the mere possession of sanctifying grace! So great is its beauty, that it not only attracts the love of the saints and angels in Heaven, but of God Himself. So great is its beauty, that the soul which possesses it is in name and in reality the friend of God and daughter of God, notwithstanding many defects and venial sins. Yes, indeed, a soul may be stained by a million venial sins; yet, if it has sanctifying grace, it will nevertheless be resplendent with such beauty as will attract the love of Almighty God, and will be regarded by Him as His most dear friend and daughter. What, then, shall we say about the beauty of a soul that keeps itself pure from the stain of even venial sin, and will not consciously allow its splendour to be dimmed by even the smallest disobedience, but studies in all things how most to please God, to the best of its power, to the best of its knowledge, desiring nothing but what God wills? Ah, the beauty of such a soul quite surpasses all human understanding! God regards it with a complacency so great, that in the sacred Canticles He thus allows the expression of His love, as it were, to burst forth : 'Thou art all fair, O My love, and there is not a spot in thee. . . . How beautiful art thou, My love, how beautiful art thou ! My friend, My dove, My sister, My spouse . . . how beautiful art thou, and how comely, My dearest, in delights !'

And this beauty, which attracts even the love of God so much—will it not suffice to attract ours? Shall we not take every possible means to acquire it ? How often those beautiful things which we greatly desire and seek after are fraught with peril ! O, how much more ought we to prize and seek after that ineffable beauty which insures all that is good for us in the sight of God !

§ 2. *In which is shown the multifarious ways in which Christian perfection is useful. First, in the testimony of a good conscience.*

Without doubt the Christian perfection of which we speak brings with it—nay, is in itself the sum and substance of all the good things which form true happiness in this life, and give the most certain hope of beatitude in the life to come. In the first place, the greatest happiness of this mortal life undoubtedly consists in the testimony of a good conscience that does not accuse us of sin. When we feel within our hearts this sweet witness we are truly happy ; and whoever is not conscious of grave faults enjoys this happiness. No one, however, can enjoy this happiness entirely and completely but those who so guard themselves against all failings that they succeed in avoiding even the slightest. The soul that has not to reproach itself with having deliberately offended against God feels an interior conviction of living for God alone ; and this is an ineffable consolation ; more particularly so if to this be superadded a constant endeavour to do what is most pleasing to God, even in things that are themselves indifferent.

§ 3. *Secondly, in the greater security of being in a state of grace.*

The Lutherans and Calvinists, &c., teach that Christians ought as firmly to believe that they are in a state of grace as they believe in the mystery of the Most Blessed Trinity. This is a stupid heresy. God has revealed that He is One God in Three Persons ; and therefore, by reason of this revelation, it is impossible that the mystery of the Blessed Trinity should not be true ; but He has never revealed to us that this person or that is in a state of grace. On the other hand, certain men of later times, who fancied that they had found the path of perfection in the wild woods of terror, taught that every soul, however good it may be, ought to live in continual anxiety, and never allow themselves to feel sure of being in a state of Divine grace, but should remain constantly suspended in a state of doubt, as in a pair of scales, until death, waiting to see at that supreme moment whether they shall fall into the embrace of Almighty God or into the arms of Satan. This also is an error. It is true that we cannot have an infallible certainty, of Divine faith, that we are in a state of grace, but we can have a presumptive certainty, which is a sufficient assurance for us, and keeps us in peace and tranquillity. Is not a son, who does not remember to have ever given grave displeasure to his father, or if he ever did so, has endeavoured to satisfy him by a true repentance, — is he not, by presumptive reasons, certain of possessing his father's love? Does he not feel so certain of it that he is able to be in peace and tranquillity? Nevertheless, he cannot have the infallible certainty of it which we have of the things that are of faith. But, setting aside a question which would take me beyond the scope of this book, who are those who can feel the most assured of possessing the infinite treasure of sanctifying grace, and thus of being the friend and son of God? Without doubt, as St. Francis of Sales assures us, they are those who fly not only from mortal sins but from venial ones also, and seek, in all things, as we have already said, that which is most pleasing to God. But, indeed, it is not necessary that St. Francis of Sales, or any other great master of spirituality, should assure us of this; for reason itself gives us sufficient evidence of the fact. Mortal sin is the turning away of our wills from the Will of God. When our wills are united with and conformed to the Will of God, mortal sin is not to be found in our souls; for union with the Divine Will is, in fact, perfect charity; and with this uniformity as the Church has defined against the blasphemies of Baius, mortal sin cannot coexist. Who, then, can feel more sure of possessing Divine grace than a soul that not only abhors mortal sins but venial sins also, and in everything tries to do what is most pleasing to God? Who can feel more secure of being in conformity with the Divine Will, and of possessing perfect charity? No one— no one certainly, although another were to work miracles, were to remove mountains, to raise the dead; for a person who is in mortal sin might work such miracles, whereas no one who possesses perfect charity can be in a state of mortal sin. Oh devout soul, is it not true that your greatest consolation would be to feel assured, as much as it is possible to be so, that you are in the grace of God; that if death should in any unexpected way or at any hour surprise you, you could not fail of reaching paradise? Well, if you would have all the security possible, you know now what you have to do—do you not? Abhor even venial sin; do in everything what is most pleasing to God, so far as you know it; and by so doing you will have more real security than you could have were you to perform the most stupendous miracles.

§ 4. *Thirdly, in the greater security of not losing the grace of God.*

One fear which torments pious souls is, that although they may be actually in a state of grace, yet they may perhaps lose it; and this fear is so great in some, that they have desired death in order to be freed from such a peril. The V. P. Paolo Segneri ordered that when the doctors should have pronounced him to be dead, notice should be given in these two lines:

'Ti rallegra, padre mio,
Non potrai più offender Dio.'

> 'Rejoice, my father,
> Thou canst not offend God any more.'

Meanwhile what souls are they that have the greatest security of not falling into mortal sin, of not losing in the future the grace of God? Certainly they are those that abhor even venial sin; for by constantly abhorring all sins, however slight, they are the more sure of abhorring grave ones. And, in fact, how would it be possible for one who fears the sting of a wasp not to fear still more the claws of a vulture? Now we know very well that the more we abhor sin, the more difficult it is for us to fall into sin. Indeed it is impossible for us to fall into sin as long as we abhor it; for sin must be voluntary in those who commit the same in order to be sin; and it cannot be voluntary in us as long as we abhor it. And is not this the greatest consolation to a soul that loves God—to a soul that desires to insure its own salvation?

I must remark, moreover, that while it is impossible to have a greater security of keeping ourselves in the grace of God than a Christian possesses who abhors every, even if it be but venial, sin, there is, on the other hand, no greater danger of losing it than that incurred by one who fears not venial sin, and consequently commits it easily and frequently. Such a one so enfeebles himself, and so chills Divine love within him, that at the shock of a violent temptation he finds himself unaccustomed to resistance, and falls miserably. This is in accordance with the words of the Holy Spirit : ' He who despises small failings will, by little and little, fall into great ones.' Following the sense of these words, St. Theresa writes, That by means of small things the demon goes on making holes through which great ones may enter ;' and terrified by the great danger, she exclaimed, ' From deliberate sin of any kind, even the smallest, may God keep you !' These truths are indeed taught, and rendered clear and palpable, by our own experience ; for we see that fervent souls who cautiously guard themselves from venial sin, although, now and then, by reason of human frailty they may fall into it, never commit mortal sin ; whereas those tepid souls who make light of venial sins, and do not endeavour to avoid them, not only commit a great number, but find themselves easily carried on into mortal sin.

§ 5. *Fourthly, through the special favour with which God regards those who aspire to Christian perfection.*

In short, what souls are they that may depend

on receiving from God the greatest abundance of grace and special predilection, if it be not those that endeavour strenuously to avoid everything which might displease Him, and always to do, so far as they know, what they believe to be most in accordance with His good pleasure? It is true that God bestows His favours gratuitously, and it is of faith that we cannot merit His grace.* Ought we not, however, to believe that in the distribution of His graces He will prefer and abundantly enrich those souls that profess for Him the greatest love and fidelity? A wise prince enriches his subjects with many gratuitous gifts, and by reason of his goodness he often gives even to the unworthy; yet who are they that enjoy the greatest amount of favour but those subjects who are the most loyal, the most faithful, and the most zealous for his honour? Ought we not to believe that in the distribution of His graces He will prefer to give most to those who prize them the most, and who try the hardest to correspond with them? Besides, though it is

* By this must be understood actual grace, or that by which He assists us to do what is good and avoid what is evil, and sanctifiying grace also, which cannot be merited by sinners who are deprived of it. As the Council of Trent teaches, it is of faith that just persons by their good works do truly deserve an increase of sanctifying grace.

true that the grace of God cannot be merited by us, yet it is equally certain that we may make ourselves unworthy of it, and put hindrances in its way. He who corresponds well with our Lord's grace is thereby in a disposition to receive more and more in future; but he who fails to correspond with it, does as much as in him lies to hinder its reception in future. So that we may well conclude in the words of Samuel: 'Cujus erunt optima quæque Israel?'—'For whom shall be all the best things of Israel?' (1 Kings ix. 20.) For whom are destined the most chosen, the most excellent gifts and graces which Almighty God grants to the children of His Church, if it be not for those who try to love Him with the greatest perfection, and to conform, at whatever cost, their own wills to the Will of God? Who, then, can ever form an idea of the supreme advantages which the Christian soul derives from the study of perfection—that is, by the avoidance even of venial sin, and by seeking in all things that which is most pleasing to God? What a treasury of good things is here collected together—a treasury of consolation, of security, of grace! Now as we have seen that the acquirement of this perfection is a thing which God requires of us all, and that it is not too difficult for us, so long as our weakness is strengthened by the omnipotent help of Divine grace, where, I would ask, is the pious and devout soul that will not feel comforted by the sweet hope of being able to obtain it, and, seeing its supernatural beauty and utility, will not feel inflamed with a great desire to follow after it, and to succeed at last in attaining it?

CHAPTER V.

ON THE MEANS OF ARRIVING AT THE MUCH-DESIRED CHRISTIAN PERFECTION.

§ 1. *The first thing to be done in order to attain Christian perfection is to desire it.*

IF I were to speak to you of all the means that might be made conducive to the attainment of Christian perfection, I should be obliged to write a very long treatise, which would be quite beyond the scope of this work, since I only propose to write a little book adapted to the capacities of all persons and to every condition of life. Not wishing, then, to deviate from the course which I laid down for myself at the beginning, I will only point out to you two methods upon which all the others usually depend. The first will put you on the path of Christian perfection; the second will serve you as a safe guide, so that you may be able to walk firmly and make rapid strides along the same road. The first is an earnest desire to attain Christian perfection; and without this desire nothing can be done. No one can learn an art who does not care to learn it, and he alone succeeds well who earnestly desires to learn his art thoroughly. If, then, you wish to arrive at Christian perfection, desire much and ardently its attainment. Do not fancy that it is pride which moves you to desire perfect sanctity. 'It is the demon,' says St. Theresa, 'who tries to make this holy desire appear to be pride.' It is not pride; it is the good will to do that which God wills us to do; for I must again repeat, His Will is our sanctification: ' Voluntas Dei sanctificatio vestra,'—' This is the Will of God, your sanctification.' Oh, that we, every one of us, had this holy pride—the holy pride of desiring to become saints!

§ 2. *This desire should be a resolve, and put immediately into execution.*

Take heed that this desire be not an irresolute desire, like the vague aspirations of many who would gladly become saints, yet never make up their minds to do so.

'These souls feed themselves on an empty desire,' says St. Alphonsus, 'but never try to make one step forward on the road to God.' 'We must begin with a fervent and steadfast resolve to give ourselves entirely to God,' says St. Francis of Sales, 'protesting before Him that for the future we desire to be His alone without any reservation; and we should go on continually renewing this same resolution.' Again observe that this resolute desire must be immediately put into execution, and not deferred ever so little. Do you not perceive how short is the period of our lives? Have we so much more time remaining, that we can afford to throw it away in useless delays and procrastinations—more particularly since we have, perhaps, already wasted much of our lives in tepidity, and may not have as much more left wherein to employ ourselves fervently in the service of God? Possibly less time remains to you than you imagine; and should the time which still remains to you prove to be short, even very short, and you meanwhile allow it to pass away without profiting by it for your sanctification, where will you get any more to make use of for your good? How wisely a certain religious lady who had been leading a careless life thought and spoke to her confessor! 'Father, I wish to become a saint, and that as soon as possible.' She was young, she enjoyed good health; she might well promise herself many years of life. Nevertheless it was soon proved that she had only a few months to live. The hour of her death was approaching, although no one suspected it. O happy one, who, having applied herself at once to the practice of Christian perfection, found that a few months sufficed for her sanctification! If she had indulged the desire only, and had deferred its execution, she would have lost the short time that remained to her; and, instead of becoming a saint, who can say how or in what state she would have gone to the other world? Besides, is not Christian perfection a treasure of beauty, and of infinite value? And why should you delay in endeavouring to acquire such a treasure? Where would you find a merchant so mad as to put off for weeks, months, or years, a lucrative stroke of business which would bring him in a hundred thousand pounds, when he could complete it at once? And here it is a question of gaining inexpressibly more than a hundred thousand pounds. Desire, then, with a true determination to become a saint, and begin immediately without any delay whatsoever, little or great.

In order to put this holy desire into practice immediately, make an entire offering of yourself to God. 'My God,' say to Him, with all your heart, 'I put myself and all I have into Thy hands, so that Thou mayest do with me what Thou willest, so that Thou mayest do with me according as it shall seem good to Thee, and in the manner Thou willest. What I hope for and desire from Thy goodness is that Thou wouldst make me holy as Thou desirest me to be, so that I may serve Thee with all perfection.' Oh, with what a sweet violence do we move the heart of God by making a full and entire offering of our souls to Him! However sinful and evil-doing the soul may have been, God cannot do otherwise than receive and bless her; nor can He refuse any of the graces necessary to make her holy. No one in the whole world can imagine how much such a soul will grow in Christian perfection, and what great things she will accomplish for the glory of God. This is not my dictum, but that of St. Ignatius of Loyola: 'Men are not aware how much they will in time accomplish for themselves and others if they abandon themselves entirely and sincerely to the Will of God.' How

HOW TO ATTAIN CHRISTIAN PERFECTION. 85

blessed would you be, O devout soul, if you would but try! What an amount of good will you begin to put into execution by this holy desire! In this offering of yourself to God really consists the secret of Christian perfection. Oh, for the love of God, and out of pity to yourselves, make this offering at once—fully and entirely—and renew it frequently. The full and entire offering of our whole self into the hands of God, who is our Father infinitely good, is exceedingly consoling even to think of. What will it be to those who have the happiness of making it in reality? What confidence, what peace, what joy, it must pour into the depths of your heart! The soul that once has the grace to make this offering fully and perfectly is, I should say, sure of becoming a saint; for it seems to me that the Divine Goodness will enfold her in such a loving embrace that God will never more allow her to fall away from Him, but will take delight in her for all eternity.

§ 3. *That we should not relax our efforts because we have not succeeded hitherto.*

Do not allow this your desire to be chilled by the pernicious thought that you have perhaps more than once before endeavoured to tread in the path of Christian perfection and have not succeeded, and that consequently you would not succeed now were you to begin again. Malignant suggestion—malignant as the demon who has caused so many to abandon themselves to a fatal despair! If you did not succeed on former occasions it was only because you had not the will to succeed. God, having given you a longing for Christian perfection, would also have given you the grace to acquire it; for He never does what is useless, and it would be useless to implant in us a good desire, and not give us the necessary grace to bring it into effect. He knows that without the assistance of His grace all our good desires would be vain; therefore He cannot give us a good desire without also giving us the grace to enable us to put it into execution. It is you who have abused this grace, and have not chosen to make use of it. If, then, you did not succeed, it was the fault of your own perverse will. Have a good will, and you will succeed. Now again God allows you to have this holy desire; and this is the forerunner of that grace which He offers you for your sanctification. Try now to desire success resolutely, profit by the grace now given you, and this time you will not fail. St. Theresa tells us 'that the Lord never ceases to favour our legitimate desires, so that we may be enabled to put them into execution' (*Foundations*). St. Alphonsus tells you that 'even if you should fall into errors a thousand times a day while endeavouring to attain Christian perfection, you must not let yourself be cast down and discouraged, but rise up again another thousand times, praying for help and resolving to fall no more. Want of confidence would be your ruin ; confidence, on the other hand, firm and unchangeable confidence, will infallibly save you, and will enable you to reach the desired perfection.' 'Let our thoughts be always elevated and full of spirit, for this shall be for our good' (St. Theresa, *Conc. dell' Amor. di Dio sop. la Cant.*). Certain people with small and feeble hearts, who live in perpetual anxiety, and, when they commit a fault, at once give themselves up almost to despair, do they not wrong the goodness of God ? Let us be humble, let us repent when we fail ; but let us not be cast down, let us never be confounded by our failures.

§ 4. *That prayer insures the efficacy of good desire.*

'Amen, amen, I say to you : If you ask the Father anything in My name He will give it you' (St. John xvi. 23). Here is a kind of promise upon oath, by which Christ Himself assures us by His own mouth that if we ask anything in His name it shall be given to us. But when is it, say the fathers, that we ask anything in the name of Jesus? It is, they answer, whenever we ask for the saving graces of eternal life. It is then that we ask in the name of Jesus, that is, in the name of our Saviour.

Observe that here our Lord Christ has pledged His own word, and contracted a real obligation with Himself, that is, with His own unfailing faithfulness. After such a promise He cannot allow us to pray in vain for any grace that we require in order to gain eternal life. Christ cannot be bound by any obligation towards us, but He can towards Himself. Now there is no grace more adapted to insure eternal life than Christian perfection; and therefore there is no grace that we can feel more sure of receiving from the Divine Goodness than this Christian perfection, if we ask for it with becoming fervour. Speaking of such prayers, St. Augustine said frankly to our Lord: 'Si has preces non audis, quas preces exaudis?'—'If Thou dost not listen to these prayers, what prayer, O Lord, wilt Thou grant?' Here, then, is the true way of rendering our good desire for Christian perfection efficacious. Without the great means of prayer, all the care, all the diligence, all the intentions in the world will be worth nothing. Prayer is worth all these things put together, because it will obtain for us all that is necessary and useful for Christian perfection.

When your soul feels itself inflamed with a strong desire to become holy, you should pray thus to the Divine Father: 'Divine Father, in the name of Jesus Christ I ask Thee to grant to me the grace to become holy. I have no need of any other, but I desire this at any cost; and steadfastly I hope to obtain it from Thy Divine goodness, since our Lord Jesus Christ Himself has given me His promise that Thou wilt grant my prayer.'

§ 5. *That the second thing to be done is to have a good spiritual director.*

Of the means that I am proposing to you, the second is one which will keep you on the true road of Christian perfection, so that you may not incline to one side or the other, and will enable you to make good use of all the remaining means necessary or opportune for the attainment of perfection; but of these I am not now speaking. It is a good director whom you ought to choose, and in all things obey. The means of acquiring perfection, besides the desire of which I have just spoken, are many and various,—prayer, vocal and mental, frequenting the most Holy Sacraments, mortification, devotion to the most Holy Mary. Nevertheless one cannot give a general rule for every one. Each one must make use of such means according to his condition and powers. One occasionally finds it stated in devout books, that those who desire to arrive at Christian perfection must frequent the most Holy Sacraments at such and such times, must make so many mental prayers and meditations, must practise such and such mortifications, &c. This is all very well, as a general principle, but not as applied to every particular case. All these are things that must be regulated according to the various conditions, capacities, and states of each person; and a good director is one who, seeing what is best suited to individual condition, capacities, and particular states, knows how to assign to each soul what she ought to do in order to arrive at perfection. He will assign one mode of life to a religious, another to a secular, another to the young unmarried woman, another to the wife, another to the shopkeeper, another to the peasant, another to the soldier, another to the learned, another to the ignorant, and so on; and thus each one, if he follow the rule set him by his director, will become a saint, although the one will not follow the same rule as the others do. From some he will require an hour of mental prayer every day; from others he would be contented with a third part of the Rosary; others he would require to frequent the Holy Sacrament once a week; to others, again, he will perhaps advise several Communions in the week; and for some he will be satisfied with a monthly Communion. In the mean time put yourself into his hands, do what he tells you to do, and you will walk securely towards the goal of Christian perfection. Observe furthermore, that if the methods of arriving at Christian perfection are various, they are not all necessary, still less are they necessary for each individual. God draws the souls of men to Him, unites them to Himself, and makes them the spouses of His love in various ways, some by greater austerity of life, some by more severe recollection and silence, some by a greater number of works of charity and of zeal. Nay, His grace, which acts with such force, but at the same time with such sweetness, knows how to adapt itself to the varied natures of different people, and, without destroying their various inclinations, bends and directs them towards the attainment of Christian perfection, as I have already shown in chap. iii. § 9. Books, however good and holy they may be, always speak generally, and cannot determine anything for one soul more than for another. It is the business of the director to give decisions and particular rules, without which general rules would remain fruitless or even hurtful, if reduced to practice without consideration and without discretion. You, then, in this very important matter of making yourself a saint, try to make use of all opportune means, but in all things follow with perfect submission and obedience him whom you have chosen to be the director of your soul.

§ 6. *Digression concerning the encouragement which this doctrine gives to devout souls.*

Permit me here to make a digression. It will be very useful, and is well adapted to the object I have in view, which is, to encourage you to aspire with success to Christian perfection. The doctrine which I have been explaining to you greatly confirms what I said as to the facility with which each individual soul may attain perfection, for we see that nothing is required of us but what every soul is able to do. Perhaps you will say to me, 'I cannot spend much time in prayer.' If it be so, spend a short time at your prayers, and that little will suffice, and Almighty God, seeing you devote to prayer what little time you are able to give, will not on account of its brevity deny you one single grace. Moreover He will bestow on you the spirit of prayer, so that you will be able to make fervent ejaculations often during the day; and at last you will pray much, though it may be interruptedly—nay, very much, almost without being aware of it.

You will, perhaps, say to me: 'I know not how to meditate, and I have never been able to learn how to do it, although I have tried with great diligence.' I understand that you are speaking of methodical and artificial meditation, in which we divide the subject by fixed points, carefully make alternate acts of the intellect and of the will, measure the time, &c.; whereas simple meditation —that is, the turning of our own thoughts to the eternal maxims—is necessary for all, every one knows how to do it, and every one can do it without exception. In fact, who does not know, who cannot reflect, that God chastises the wicked, that God rewards the good, that for the love of us He became incarnate, that He suffered for us, &c.? You are speaking, then, of methodical and artificial meditation. You know not how to do it, and cannot learn how? If this be true, it means that for you it is not necessary, and you shall hear presently what St. John of the Cross says on this subject.

Again, you may say to me: 'I cannot frequent the most Holy Sacraments very often. My occupations, or my husband, or my parents do not allow it.' If this be true, do so by desire: take care to avoid sin, that you may not have need of frequent Confession; make spiritual Communions, and God will make them supply the place of sacramental Communions. If it were impossible for you to frequent the Sacraments more than once a year, that would suffice to make you holy; nay, you could become a saint even if you could not receive them once in the year, as is the case with not a few Christians living in the desert wilds of Asia, Africa, and America, who have not a single priest permanently resident among them.

Or you may say to me: 'I cannot undertake spiritual reading, such as the Lives of the Saints, books concerning perfection, &c., because I have not time to do so.' If what you say is true, be contented with listening on holy-days to the Divine words of the Gospel, and the instruction you will thus receive will be sufficient instruction for you. And should you reply that you cannot even listen to the Divine word, because you are so unfortunate as to have irreligious parents or an irreligious husband who will not allow you to listen to preaching nor to be present at Catechism, lay your wants before God, and pray that He will not leave you without the bread of spiritual instruction. He is a good Father, and will provide for your necessities. Be tranquil and peaceful meanwhile, remembering that, so long as this impossibility lasts, neither spiritual reading nor listening to the Divine word are at all necessary for your growth in Christian perfection, because Almighty God will supply the deficiency in other ways, by means of His Divine inspirations and illuminations, sent directly from Himself or by means of your guardian angel.

You will say perhaps to me : 'I am not able to bear retirement, silence, or an austere life.' If it be so, it only means that you are not by nature adapted for a monastic life, retired from the world, nor for the rigorous discipline of a very mortified life. Provided you take care to avoid all sinful or dangerous company, conversation, places of meeting, amusements; provided you keep guard over your tongue, so that it does not transgress by words offensive either to religion, to charity, or to good morals; provided you mortify your passions so far as they are inordinate, and observe the abstinence prescribed by Holy Church,—you may become a saint. Instead of distinguishing yourself by the virtues of retirement, of silence, of penitence, the grace of God, accommodating itself to your disposition and temperament, will cause you to be distinguished in other ways, such as affability, gentleness, obedience, justice, &c. In short, whatever you may tell me, provided you avoid even venial sins—and that in things which we should call indifferent, you choose what you know to be most pleasing to God—then in whatsoever way, according to your power, you may exercise yourself in the practice of the means for attaining Christian perfection, you will become holy. Now tell me—if this doctrine is not consoling, what is?

But is it all equally certain? I defy you to find any argument capable of throwing a doubt upon it. Nevertheless, in order to make you see with your own eyes that this doctrine is not mine only, but that of the saints, listen to one of the greatest masters of spiritual life who ever adorned the Church of God, namely, St. John of the Cross. He represents the Divine Spouse as saying to the soul He has espoused (*Trat. delle Spine*, coll. 7):

'If My servants would observe My ways attentively they would see that not one but many are the roads by which I guide souls to Myself, and would consider that the Heavenly Jerusalem has not one but twelve gates, and would remember that in the house of My Father there are not one but many mansions, and would bear in mind how the varying soil of their hearts yields various kinds of fruit; they would not vainly toil to lead every soul by one road, bring them all in at one door, and lodge them all in one place, requiring from all the same kind of fruit. Do you not remember that, in dividing My talents and My graces, I gave to one person one talent, to another two talents, to the third five talents? It is to no purpose that some of My servants busy themselves in demanding two talents of prayer from those to whom I have given but one, and five from those to whom I have given only two. My call is more powerful than that of man, and they do little good to souls who persist in calling to them to travel on one road, when I have invited them to come to Me by another.'

From all this it must be concluded that we should not exact any particular practice from every one, provided it be not commanded; that we must observe what the capacity of each one is able to bear, and, according to such capacity, direct each soul towards the attainment of perfection.

To descend to a particular example: what practice is more useful for the attainment of perfection than prayer by meditation? And yet is it not certain that meditation must not be required from every one? Let us hear again what St. John of the Cross says in the above-quoted work (coll. 8). It is the Divine Spouse who is speaking: 'The first road is that of vocal prayer. To whomsoever I will I commit one talent, and so good a one that, if he has the wisdom to trade with it, he will gain Heaven. There are some people, and they are not few in number, whose souls are at once excited to devotion by reciting the Rosary and other prayers, or by making devout ejaculations; but as soon as they have closed their lips their hearts close up also, and become cold again. Now such people should follow this road of vocal prayer, and their confessor should help them to do it. . . .

'If you cannot meditate, O My daughter, do not desire to do what I do not will that you should do; for if you desire what is contrary to My Will your desire will not be fulfilled, and this nonfulfilment will be a torment to you. Begin, then, by desiring what I desire and you shall obtain it, and it will bring you peace. If I give you not these two talents, would you wrest them from Me by force?' (He says that two talents are given to those who possess the gift of meditation.) 'No, certainly not; humble yourself, and take what I offer, which most certainly is better for you than what you long for.'

Now I do not therefore wish you to suspect me of holding any religious practices, or any means conducive to perfection, to be of little account, particularly that of methodical meditation, of which St. John of the Cross here speaks. I esteem them all exceedingly, especially that methodical meditation so much recommended by masters of spirituality; but at the same time, as I had proposed to myself to convince and persuade you that for the perfection of each particular soul nothing is required that each cannot accomplish, I could not do less than warn you that not all the means conducive to Christian perfection are necessary for its attainment. Moreover I wished to bring before you in preference to any other an authority so decisive as that of the above-named saint, in order to make it perfectly understood that souls must not advance whither it seems best or most agreeable to them, but rather let themselves be sweetly guided along that road to which the Spirit of God calls them. It is useful and necessary to put a force upon ourselves in order to bridle and conquer our inordinate passions, for we should constrain ourselves to be obedient, chaste, gentle, and so on; but it is not useful, it is not necessary for the purpose of intruding ourselves into those paths of perfection which we are not called to tread. For this reason we should not force ourselves into methods of prayer for which we have not strength, or into a manner of life for which we are not by nature formed. But meanwhile, who can safely decide in his own cause about his own capacity, ability, strength, reasonable inclinations, &c.? No soul can decide for herself; and here we see the necessity of allowing ourselves to be directed and regulated by our spiritual director, who, being illuminated by God, will know what we are able to perform, and what we ought to do with regard to the various means of attaining perfection.

§ 7. *The necessity of obedience to our spiritual director.*

Obedience is the virtue which is required from you first of all, in order that you may profit by the spiritual suggestions and rules given to you by your director. If you are among the number of those persons who aspire to Christian perfection, and who are yet disobedient to their directors, woe betide you! Instead of becoming more perfect, you will grow worse from day to day. Be obedient, be perfectly obedient. Do not flatter yourself that you can ever arrive at sanctity if you indulge the vice of disobedience. Can it be possible that, knowing the foundation of all saintliness to be humility, you will presume to put for its foundation in yourself the most evil of all the daughters of pride, which is disobedience? Guard yourself also from the pretension, so full of pride, that you understand the reasons why you are commanded or forbidden certain things; guard yourself from the diabolical suspicion that perhaps your director does not understand you, or does not fully know you. He is illuminated by God; you should understand this to be the reason why he commands or prohibits, and you should not try to understand any other. Our Lord enables him to know and comprehend the state of your conscience. If he did not know and fully understand it, he would prescribe nothing. What he prescribes to you he prescribes precisely because he knows you, because he understands you. These pretensions and suspicions are the origin of the most fatal disobedience. It would seem impossible that certain souls, who desire to be devout, should allow themselves to be so drawn aside as they are by Satan, by the great demon of pride, to disobey their director continually, and that while they are scrupulous in everything else, never have scruples at all about the continual disobedience in which they are living. The Pope himself, the Vicar of Christ, the head and ruler of all the Catholic Church, who has such depth of doctrine, such light, such authority to rule over all the bishops and all the faithful of the Catholic world,—the Pope himself must submit in that which regards his own conscience, and perfectly obey his spiritual director. With such an example before you, can you allow yourself to be so proud that you do not choose to obey? As if this would be the way to make ourselves saints! Oh, may God preserve us from imitating such disobedient souls!

And in what should you be obedient? The answer can be given in one sentence. In all things concerning your soul; concerning the things of which you ought to accuse yourself, or ought not to accuse yourself, in Confession; concerning the

Communions which you should make, whether more or less frequent; concerning your prayers and other devout practices, which you should undertake and which leave alone; concerning the mortifications which you should or should not practise; and so on. You should obey in all these, and in all similar things which concern the guidance of your soul. Mark well this saying of St. Theresa: 'The devil, knowing that no road leads us so quickly to the highest perfection as that of obedience, places in your way many difficulties and annoyances under the guise of what is good' (*Foundations*). Therefore if you also, under the pretence of some greater good, should be tempted to disobey, reject the diabolical suggestion.

§ 8. *In which it is shown that it is not too difficult a thing to find a good director, and that if we do not, God Himself will supply the need.*

This director, however, ought to be a good one; and this is the great point, you will say—this is the great difficulty, to find a good director Nevertheless do not be frightened at this either. We have seen that it is not too difficult a thing to arrive at Christian perfection; and yet if it were too difficult a thing for us to find a good director, it must also be too difficult to attain Christian perfection. And here I will first ask you whether you are living in a place where there are many confessors, out of whom you may choose one, or whether you are in a place where there is but one only, and where you must be contented with this one? If you are living in a place where there is one confessor only, and where, by reason of the distance, you cannot apply to any other, then this one confessor will for you be a good one, since Almighty God, seeing your good intention, your earnest desire to become holy, will make him be good for you, even if he be not a good director in himself. Such a one is, often and often, like those of whom the Prophet speaks: 'Linguas infantium fecit disertas' (Wisdom x. 21),—'Wisdom . . . made the tongues of infants eloquent.' He to whom it costs nothing to make inexperienced children speak wisely, when their words contribute to His glory, cannot find any difficulty in causing one of His ministers to speak well and wisely for your spiritual good, although he may not naturally be very well instructed or experienced. When a soul presents herself for confession with a good will to the minister of God before whom he is able to appear, then that minister of God does not speak of himself; God suggests to him the sentiments he utters, God makes him speak; and in this way he speaks as a wise and learned man, he speaks as a saint, although in himself he may be neither the one nor the other. Cornelius à Lapide, commenting on the Book of Wisdom i. 1, 'In simplicitate cordis quærite illum,' quotes a saying reputed to be of the Blessed Dorotheus, in the following words: God will not allow those to be in want of a spiritual director who in all simplicity seek God alone and the fulfilment of His holy Will; and if there be no director at hand to instruct them, He will supply the want even by means of a child, to whom He will give light and prudence for that end. If, then, you have no choice, and are obliged to content yourself with such or such a confessor, be satisfied; he will guide you well, because Almighty God will not allow him to guide you ill.

Should you object, that souls most desirous of perfection have sometimes been somewhat unfortunate in their choice of a director, and that God allowed such a one to commit some negligence or imprudence in directing them—an occurrence which St. Theresa lamented, and like what happened to St. Jane Frances de Chantal—if you bring forward these arguments against me, I answer, that often our

Lord allows devout souls to suffer minor evils, in order to bring a greater good out of them. He therefore permits these great souls accidentally to fall in with directors who are in some way or other inefficient, and He also permits them to feel in some degree the effects of this inefficiency, so that they may become more experienced in choosing a director for themselves in future, and that they may profit by their experience for the benefit of those innumerable souls who will come to them for counsel and guidance. So that the harm experienced is slight, and in the sight of God perhaps rather imaginary than real, while the good they derive for themselves and for others is considerable. Never suppose for a moment that God will permit those souls who go to Him with sincerity, and truly seek His love, to suffer from any evils or mistakes, except for their greater advantage, or for their more appreciable instruction. If this were to happen with regard to yourself, would you not be satisfied?

§ 9. *When among various directors a selection can be made, we ought then to choose one of the best. Suggestions are made for instruction on this head.*

Besides, there are very few people who find themselves under the necessity of applying to one fixed director only, without choice of any other. In cities, in tolerably populous country parishes, there is always a variety of confessors; and where there is only one in a parish, we may have recourse to one or other in the neighbourhood; for there is not a doubt that, where we can, we ought to make a selection, and not take the first we meet. Confessors may all be good, but it is very certain that all confessors are not equally good. Confessors are like doctors, they are all supposed to be skilful in healing maladies, but yet all are not equally practical or learned in their science. Now, as we believe it to be our duty to choose for ourselves a doctor from among those who have the greatest reputation, and are the best for the cure of our temporal infirmities, should we not with greater reason believe ourselves to be under the obligation of choosing a confessor from among the most enlightened and the best for the cure of our spiritual infirmities?

But how can shopkeepers, women, girls, in their simplicity and perhaps also their ignorance and want of cultivation, discern and select a good confessor? It seems difficult, but they can find him if they determine to do so; and if you, my reader, are among the number of these, do you, in making your selection, begin by recommending yourself to God, and rest assured that He will supply all that you are unable of yourself to accomplish. The best thing would be that you should make a Novena to the Holy Ghost; and pray for the intercession of the most Holy Mary and of your guardian angel. You will see that by seeking a good spiritual director in this manner you will not fail of success. Remember also the similitude in the holy Gospels, where it is written, 'Every good tree yieldeth good fruit, and the bad tree yieldeth bad fruit.' The life and works of the ministers of God enlighten us much as to whether they are truly good and to be trusted with the direction of our souls. I am supposing, besides, that you live where all the confessors are good—where they may all be compared to good trees bearing good fruit. But as you have to choose from among them the best among the good, reflect that if good trees bring forth good fruit, so it is equally true that the better trees bring forth the better fruit. Among the confessors who are put before you for selection you ought to prefer one of those who, by their good works and by their edifying priestly conduct, are distinguished among the good. Therefore make your choice among those who celebrate Mass with the greatest devotion, who have the greatest spirit of prayer—who have the reputation of the greatest learning—who if they do preach (for among the best confessors there are some who do not preach at all) show the greatest fervour and zeal for the salvation of souls, and who, being entirely occupied in the exercise of their ministry, are detached from the life and pleasures of the world. Among these you will find not only good but even the best confessors; among these you are sure of making a good choice. Then, when you have found a good spiritual director, do not change him without a reasonable motive, but look upon him as another angel whom God has sent you, and who, together with your guardian angel, should conduct you to Paradise.

It would be also well that you should declare to him your earnest desire to become holy. 'Father,' you will say to him, 'hitherto I have been careless in the service of our Lord, and did not think of my sanctification; but now that our Lord has enlightened me, and made known to me the great wrong that I have committed in loving so little a God who is all goodness—now I wish to attend with all diligence to my sanctification, and

I beg of your fatherly kindness to assist and guide me in the new life which I intend to undertake.' Your director will feel the more encouraged to suggest to you all that he may consider most conducive for your perfection: therefore do not omit, for the sake of a humility that would be false, or for the sake of a shyness that would be irrational, to lay bare before him your good resolution.

§ 10. *Model of a good director.*

If you wish besides to have before you the model of a good director, on whom you may model your own choice of one, I will put one before you, and then I will conclude.

But who, indeed, shall I choose among all the excellent spiritual directors that adorn the Church of God? A thousand come before my mind, all admirable and all safe. But—asking pardon of all the others—the one who, at the present moment, especially attracts my admiration is the very dear St. Philip Neri. Setting aside the extraordinary gifts with which he was enriched in abundance, and which we cannot pretend to find in our own director, here is the prototype of confessors.

So ardent was his zeal for hearing confessions,

that he shut himself up in the confessional even when none presented themselves for Confession, in the hope that some poor sinful man or woman, seeing the opportunity, would chance to profit by it. When any one at last came, he showed himself so ready that he would leave off the recital of his Office at any part of it, so as not to keep the penitent waiting even the shortest time. His manners were always sweet and gentle—indeed one may say joyous, and his heart so large that it might be described as being like that of Solomon, 'sicut arena quæ est in litore maris,'—'like the sand on the sea-shore.' So that among those who had recourse to him the most afflicted were consoled, the most agitated became tranquil, the most timid were comforted, the most despairing found hope revive within them. He infused into his penitents the great idea that he possessed of the Divine Goodness; he enkindled in them the holy love which burned so strongly in him, and by means of this burning love worked in them all that was necessary for their salvation. Hence he was the greatest enemy to scruples, and to all the subtlety and diffidence which they bring, with such fatal effect, to the hindrance of Christian perfection. Hence he was most averse to rigorous maxims, that only serve to chill Divine love in the most well-intentioned persons, and cause them to forget that God is our Father. His pliant spirit bent itself to sympathise with all the inclinations, with all the tendencies, of the nature and condition of every person, so that he drew them all, without constraint or violence, to God. He was learned with the learned, ignorant with the ignorant, a child with children, 'omnibus omnia factus,'—'all things to all men,' as St. Paul says. So jealous was he of virginal purity, that though he had been confessor for a space of not less than thirty years to a lady celebrated in Rome for her rare beauty, he yet did not know her by sight. He lived so detached from the love of temporal things that he even sold his books, to give the value of them in alms. His devotion to our Blessed Lady was so great that, even when he was ill, he passed whole nights in such sweet colloquy with her, that those who attended upon him from sunset to daybreak were scarcely aware of the swift passage of all these long hours; and it sometimes happened that they mistook the morning Angelus for that of the preceding evening. Here you have before you a miraculous prototype of a spiritual director. I do not say that you should seek for one who would be his equal, because that would be too difficult to find. But you should look for one who in some degree may resemble him in these points, which are of such vital importance.

CONCLUSION.

AND now, devout soul, I have finished the little work that I undertook for your consolation, in order to encourage and direct you a short way on the path of Christian perfection. Oh, if I could but persuade you that God desires you to be holy, not merely with the simple holiness which consists in being pure from mortal sin, but with the perfected sanctity which consists in the perfect union of our wills with the Divine Will! Oh, that you were persuaded that this sanctity is not too difficult of attainment; that there is nothing in Heaven or earth which possesses greater beauty or greater usefulness!—that you were more resolute in adopting those means which would secure to you the possession of it! If you do not feel sufficiently persuaded—sufficiently resolved, read over again this little book, praying our Lord meanwhile to suggest to your hearts these desires, and to illumine your mind with that light which I have been unable to give or suggest in this little book of mine. Pray to our Lady to intercede for you; and as in these desires and in this Divine illumination consists true wisdom, repeat, until she grants your prayer,

'Sedes Sapientiæ, ora pro nobis.'

Meanwhile have the charity to recompense the good intention with which I have written this little book by reciting for me an Ave Maria.

APPENDIX.

WHAT SORT OF IDEA THE DEVOUT SOUL SHOULD TAKE CARE TO HAVE ABOUT THE HOLY FEAR OF GOD.

'I ENTREAT you, my dear daughter, for the honour of God, do not be afraid of God, for He could in no way wish to bring the smallest evil upon you. On the contrary, love Him much, because He desires to do you the greatest good.' Thus writes St. Francis of Sales to a devout soul (*Spir. Letters*, p. 2). These words, if they had not been written by a saint, might scandalise many persons, and particularly devout souls. 'St. Francis of Sales,' they would say, 'disapproves, then, of the fear of God— of that fear which is the beginning of wisdom, which is a gift of the Holy Spirit. And can he be a saint who begs and entreats a devout soul not to fear God?' And nevertheless these words are worthy of a saint, and of a saint so celebrated in spiritual science as St. Francis of Sales; and you should allow me to repeat them to you also. Do not think that St. Francis of Sales disapproves of the fear of God—of that fear which is the beginning of wisdom, which is the gift of the Holy Spirit. He disapproves of the fear which is born of distrust, which brings with it disquietude, which instead of honouring God dishonours Him; and therefore he begs us for the honour of God not to fear God in this manner. And this fear, which is born of distrust, which brings disquietude, which does no honour to God, is that which I desire, O devout soul, to take from you, because it can do you no good, but on the contrary may do you much harm.

The holy fear of God is the foundation and the base of Christian perfection, and for this reason it is most necessary for souls even the most devout and most saintly; for this reason those false mystics are justly condemned who teach that the fear of God is opposed to the perfection of charity—that is, to the love of God; for this reason I desire that the fear of God may always accompany you, so that through it you may always be preserved from sin. You must, however, have a just idea of this holy fear. If you have this just idea of it you will be powerfully assisted thereby in the acquirement of Christian perfection; otherwise you will find yourself cowardly, distrustful, intimidated, terrified—without peace in your heart. Hearken, then, to what it should be.

§ 1. *The holy fear of God ought to be a calm and tranquil fear.*

The fear of God is of two kinds—servile and filial. We have a servile fear when we fear to offend God on account of the chastisement with which He punishes sin. When you fear to commit or to have committed any mortal sin because you are threatened with hell-fire and the loss of paradise, this is servile fear; and although this fear is not of perfection, and is properly not one of the seven gifts of the Holy Spirit, yet it is a good and salutary fear as defined by the Council of Trent (Sess. vi. c. 6); nay, it is a movement of the Holy Spirit (Sess. xiv. c. 4).

We have a filial fear when we fear to offend God on account of the displeasure caused to Him by our sins, fearing to insult and offend a goodness so great that it merits infinite love. This is a fear truly perfect; this is properly one of the sevenfold gifts of the Holy Spirit (St. Thom. xxii. q. 19, a. 9). Now, whether servile or filial, the holy fear of God comes from the Spirit of God;

but the Spirit of God is the Spirit of peace, of order, of tranquillity, and cannot be a spirit of disturbance, of confusion, of disorder. Hence as a natural consequence the holy fear which it inspires must be peaceful, well ordered, tranquil; and whenever you find that the fear of death, of the Divine judgment, and of hell disturbs you, confounds you, upsets you, so that you are deprived of peace, you should then judge that it is not a good fear, inspired by God. This is a rule approved by all the spiritual masters, particularly St. Ignatius of Loyola and St. Francis of Sales.

§ 2. *When the fear of God is not tranquil, it impedes what is good, and may do much evil.*

Reflect now a little and with attention how spiritual things fare with you when you are agitated by inordinate fears and terrors. Is it not true that then your prayers are dry and distracted, so that you do not feel the usual consolation, and do not derive from it that vigour of resolution and purpose which you gain when you have prayed with a tranquil heart and a serene mind? Is it not true that confidence in obtaining the graces you ask for is wanting? Is it not true that the greater and more important these graces are so much the more your confidence diminishes? And then what pitiable misery you endure when you approach the Blessed Sacrament! With these continual fears that you are not sufficiently well prepared, that you are not in proper dispositions, you lose yourself in so many useless thoughts and searchings and self-examinations that your soul becomes completely crushed—deprived of the consolation and of the strength which the fervour of a quiet and peaceful contrition gives. Hence when you approach the most august Sacrament, how the cruel thought that perhaps you are stained with hidden mortal sin, and are consequently in disfavour with our Lord Jesus, whom you are receiving into your heart, afflicts you, hinders your devotion, and extinguishes the affections of Divine love! And may it not happen at last that you become weary of a devout life, because you find in it nothing but disquietude and bitterness—that you become negligent in prayer, and keep away from the most Holy Sacraments, as so many others have done, after having allowed themselves to be overwhelmed by excessive fears and tormenting disquietude? Fly from such a danger as this, and preserve your tranquillity of heart.

§ 3. *On the means for preserving tranquillity of heart.*

If you are among the number of those souls that are too much cast down by the contemplation of Almighty God in His attribute of infinite justice, fix your gaze for the future on that of His infinite goodness. Generally speaking we ought to look upon Him sometimes from the one side and sometimes from the other; because God desires to be feared as well as loved, and consequently the severity of His judgments, as well as the tenderness of His mercy, ought to be the object of our contemplation. But you must observe that whereas in estimating the love of God we cannot exceed, we cannot assign to it any measure, or as St. Bernard says: 'Modus diligendi Deum est diligere sine modo,'—'The measure of our love of God should be to love Him without measure'—in the fear of God we may easily fall into excess, and pass those bounds of moderation which a filial and confiding love necessitates. Hence when a soul has a sufficient fear of God, and this fear still goes on increasing, till it deprives the heart of peace and the mind of serenity, that soul should not endeavour to increase the fear still more by considerations of the Divine justice and chastisements; but, on the contrary, should try to moderate it, and to grow in the confidence which a holy love inspires by reflecting upon the goodness and mercy of God. Therefore the Passion of our Lord, the most Holy Sacrament of the Altar, the mercy of God, paradise, the benefits you have already received from God, and suchlike things which fill the heart with confidence and love, should be the objects of your contemplation; but considerations on hell, judgment, and suchlike things you should lay aside until you have regained tranquillity of heart; and therefore you should not put yourself in the way of hearing sermons on these subjects, nor of reading those books which treat of them.

Perhaps you will say, 'The Holy Ghost exhorts us to consider the last four things, among which there is the judgment and there is hell; and yet you tell me that I ought to abstain from such subjects of contemplation?' I answer that it is your duty to abstain from them, because the Holy Spirit, in giving this exhortation, speaks generally to all Christians. It is a general rule which admits of exceptions; of which exception you are an example, by reason of your spiritual weakness, which produces in you excessive fear and consternation when you contemplate these truths. The Holy Ghost, in more than one part of the Divine Scriptures, teaches us that wine revives and strengthens man; and this is a truth which one cannot doubt. But it is a general rule only; and in fact if you were to give it to the majority of sick people, instead of strengthening you would destroy them. Here, then, we have a particular example.

Does this doctrine of mine appear strange to you? Read the seventh colloquy, n. 4, of the *Trattate Delle Spine* of St. John of the Cross, and you will find that this great master of spirituality does not hesitate to teach that some souls are not called by God to meditate on the four last things; and that therefore those teachers labour in vain who try to lead by the path of fear certain souls who cannot do anything except through love, because such is the Divine Will. Read also what St. Francis of Sales says (*Letters*, book iii. lett. 19): 'Do not be careful to read those parts of a book where death, judgment, and hell are enlarged upon, because you, by the grace of God, being firmly established in a Christian mode of life, do not require to be induced by means of horror and terror to embrace it.' Thus, then, you perceive that

THE HOLY FEAR OF GOD. 123

in no way have I departed from the doctrine of the saints. But let us listen furthermore to a little theological reasoning. Is not the love of God sufficient to make us saints? Without doubt it is sufficient; and while nothing suffices for our sanctification if it be not accompanied by Divine love, this Divine love suffices of itself alone, although everything else be wanting. Therefore, I say, considerations on the life, passion, and death of our Lord Jesus Christ, of the immense and innumerable benefits which He has given us, of the glory which He has prepared for us, — will not these suffice to enkindle in us the most perfect love of God? And with this love burning within us, what more do we require to become saints? And I should not wish any one to suppose that considerations on the Divine benefits towards us are but little adapted to enkindle in our hearts the perfect love of God—thinking that from these considerations usually proceed those sentiments only of Divine love which theologians call of concupiscence or of hope. Not so; for when we consider the beneficence of God towards His creatures, we begin also to understand more clearly how good He is in Himself; and hence, added to the love that is born of hope, by which we love God because He is good to us, there speedily comes in its train that perfect love called the love of friendship, by which we love God because He is infinitely good in Himself, and thus the perfection of charity is formed within us. This is the doctrine of St. Thomas. St. Ignatius also, putting before us, in the book of his Exercises, considerations to excite in the soul the perfect love of God, makes use of the recollection of the Divine benefits as one of the most efficacious means to enkindle in our hearts perfect charity.

And I therefore exhort you to exercise yourself in this consideration—the recollection of God's benefits—in preference to all others. It reminds us of our creation, of our preservation by a protecting Providence, of our vocation to the faith, of the passion and death of our Saviour, of the institution of the most Holy Sacraments, &c., memories which of themselves are enough to inspire gratitude, hope, consolation, and the most perfect love. Yet you will say to me that the holy fear of God is the beginning of wisdom—that is, of Christian perfection; and this I admit also, otherwise I should be falling into a contradiction of the Divine Word of God. But have you not the fear of God already? Have you it not even to excess—to such excess that it causes you disturbance and disquietude? Yes, you already possess it. Then there is no necessity that you should go on seeking for that which you already possess. Perhaps you may reply, ' I might lose it were I to leave off exercising myself in those thoughts which keep it up.' Be tranquil. As long as you possess the holy love of God you cannot possibly be wanting in a holy fear of Him; because whosoever loves God necessarily fears to offend God, necessarily dreads hell, which is the eternal separation from Him, and in which the greatest of all its miseries is to hate God. Observe well this truth: the fear of God may exist in our souls without the love of Him; this is the case with those who repent of their sins from attrition only; but the love of God can never exist unaccompanied by a holy fear. And moreover I do not wish in the least to teach you that you ought to forget those truths of religion which serve to excite in our hearts the fear of God; only I would say to you that so long as the spiritual infirmity remains by reason of which you suffer excessive apprehension and lose peace, so long you should abstain from the consideration of those beforenamed truths, and not resume them until, being well founded in confidence towards God, you still fear God indeed, but in a calm and tranquil manner, as the best of fathers would desire to be feared by his children.

§ 4. *We ought not to lose tranquillity of heart because we commit faults and even sins.*

Here I might write much, and make you see at a glance that it is no virtue to be confounded and overwhelmed with apprehensions after having committed sins, or after having been betrayed into faults—that it is even the result of a certain secret pride, as all the masters of spirituality agree. But I will merely ask you if you have ever read, or heard it said, that confusion, sinking of heart, and terror cancel in us the defects and sins of the soul? Have you anywhere read or heard such a thing mentioned? No, certainly not. Defects and sins are cancelled by sorrow and by repentance; so that if you fall into any fault, even a grievous one (from which may God guard you, and from which He will certainly guard you if you desire always to love Him), humble yourself, repent, but with peacefulness and with tranquillity of heart; for this is certainly the way to obtain mercy and to be sure of amendment. What pity those souls inspire who on the smallest occasion become beside themselves, disconcerted, confounded! An imperfection alone is sufficient to make them run confused and terrified to their confessor, so that he is actually unable to pacify them. What possible benefit can be expected from these excesses of terror and apprehension?

§ 5. *We ought not to lose tranquillity of heart on account of the uncertainty of remaining in a state of grace.*

Although in chapter iv. § 3 I have already pointed out that we may have a true certainty of being in the grace of God, when we either do not remember to have committed mortal sin, or when, having committed it, we have done our best to obtain pardon, nevertheless, as this is a point seldom or never elucidated in books on spirituality, which is of the greatest importance for the peace of souls, and is by many wrongly understood, I consider it necessary to recur to it again, and expound the true and safe doctrine.

As we may see in the writings of Cardinal Bellarmine (*On Justification*, book iii. c. ix. &c.), who treats at length on this controversy against the heretics, the most holy Council of Trent has defined that we cannot be certain, with the infallible certainty of faith, that we are in the grace of God. This is most certain by the infallible authority of the Council, and also evident for theological reasons. For no truth can be of faith if it be not a revealed truth; and Almighty God has never revealed to the Holy Catholic Church the particular state of souls—whether such and such souls are or are not in a state of grace. But further, while it says that we cannot be certain with the certainty of infallible faith that we are in the grace of God, it does not say that we are uncertain —that is, that we should live in a state of perpetual doubt as to whether we are or are not the friends of God. We Genoese know certainly that Genoa exists. But do we know it with the infallible certainty of faith? Certainly not; for God has never revealed to us the existence of the city of Genoa; we know it by physical certainty, so long as we see it and are within its walls. We know also for a certainty that London, Paris, Milan, Naples, &c., exist, but we know this only (never having seen these cities) with a moral and human certainty, because we are told and made sure in so many ways that these cities really do exist. A friend is certain of being loved by his friend, but he is certain by a presumptive certainty, because he has so many proofs and arguments in favour of the affection of this friend. Here, then, we are certain of many things, although we do not believe them with the Divine and infallible faith with which we believe in the verities revealed by God; so, then, in the same manner, with the certainty of a human, moral, and presumptive faith, we may feel sure of being in the grace of God. These are the precise terms used by Cardinal Bellarmine in the above-mentioned passage : 'certitudo conjecturalis, certitudo humana et moralis non fidei,'—' presumptive human and moral certainty, not the certainty of faith.' This, then, explains why we may, with a real certainty, feel assured that we are in a state of grace, because *human, moral, presumptive certainty* is true certainty. Hence, when we read that man is not certain of being in the grace of God, we ought to understand it as meaning that certainty of infallible faith which is only to be found in revealed truth ; but meanwhile, humanly speaking, we are able always to feel assured that we are friends of God, provided we are not aware of having ever committed a mortal sin, or, having done so, have sincerely repented of it. You, devout soul, are certainly either among the number of those who are not aware of having ever grievously offended God, or among those who have already begun to detest their grave sins. You can then feel sure of enjoying the friendship of God, and you should avoid that feeling of uncertainty which would tend to destroy the peace of your soul.

§ 6. *Neither should we lose this tranquillity from a dread of hidden mortal sin.*

But perhaps you will answer me, that you may be lying under the guilt of some hidden mortal sin, and hence find yourself out of God's grace without knowing it. But I reply that this dread of hidden mortal sin in souls that desire to love God, and consequently do their best to love Him, is a mere phantom. It is certain that souls who live forgetful of God, of themselves, and of eternity may very easily be guilty of hidden sins that are even mortal. It is certain that even pious souls have hidden venial sins, and hence we should say with David: 'Ab occultis meis munda me Domine,'—'From my secret sins cleanse me, O Lord' (Ps. xviii. 13). The first have hidden sins, possibly mortal ones, because they neglect prayer and the Word of God; hence they fail seriously in their duties by reason of culpable blindness and ignorance. The second have hidden venial sins, because on account of human weakness and infirmity they are guilty of many shortcomings of which they are not fully aware, of which the Scriptures say, 'septies enim cadet justus,'—'a just man shall fall seven times.' But the souls that desire to love God, who pray, and frequent the Sacraments, and listen to the Divine word, can they be committing hidden mortal sins? Let us reason out the question theologically. Sin cannot be mortal unless it be deliberate, either in itself or in the cause of it. That ignorance which is seriously culpable must also be a deliberate and conscious ignorance. If the sin be deliberate, and the person who commits it be fully conscious of it, it can no longer be a hidden sin. How, indeed, would it be possible for me to eat flesh-meat on a Friday, knowing that I am doing a thing gravely prohibited, and yet not know that I had sinned? This sin could not be hidden from me; it would be most manifest. Moreover can mortal sins be hidden when they proceed from seriously culpable ignorance, such as is found in those who violate the precepts of the law of God or of the Church, because they do not care to be instructed in the same? Such ignorance cannot have any place in you; and then, do you not frequent sermons and Christian instructions? Yes, no doubt; then you must be well acquainted with your duties. But if you happen to be accidentally ignorant on one point, and hence fail in that particular, this ignorance in you would be a guiltless ignorance, because unintentional, and the fault you committed in consequence could not in any way be a mortal sin, since it never can happen that a person sins by misfortune and without malice. Yet such would be the case if a person could be in mortal sin through being unconsciously ignorant of some particular point of duty, while all the time trying his best to acquaint himself thoroughly with his duties. Courage, then; banish for ever this spectre of hidden mortal sin. St. Francis of Sales, St. Theresa, St. Alphonsus, and all the good masters of spirituality teach you that mortal sin is a horrible monster, which cannot enter into a soul that fears God without that soul being clearly aware of it.

Nevertheless I will for a moment suppose that you are guilty of some hidden mortal sin, of which you are not aware, and consequently have no intention of repenting and confessing it. You are then guilty of this hidden mortal sin? Well, for how long a time will it burden you? 'For ever,' you will say, 'until I become aware of it, repent of it, and confess it.' Are you talking this nonsense seriously? Let us reason again, and bring a little theology to bear upon it. It is a doctrine of the Catholic Church that perfect charity cannot coexist with mortal sin, and the contrary opinion is condemned among other blasphemies of Baius. Hence all the Catholic theologians teach that an act of the love of God which is made by the soul when it loves God above all things, because He is infinitely good, cancels any mortal sin whatever, even if it were a reserved case for the Papal absolution only, and cancels it because an act of pure love of God contains in itself contrition for sin, and the vow, or at all events the desire, for the Sacrament of Confession. Consequently though you are guilty of a hidden mortal sin, so serious a one that only the Pope himself could absolve you—nay, though you are guilty of a hundred, of a thousand such—if you make an act of the love of God, by reciting from the heart an act of charity, and, still better, of contrition, all will be cancelled, and you will immediately be in the grace of God—it being understood of course that the obligation would remain with you of confessing such sins if, in the lapse of time, you should know or discover them. Now therefore, even if you should have the guilt of some unknown mortal sin upon your soul, it will not weigh you down nor drag you into disfavour with Almighty God until the time arrives that you become aware of such sin, and you repent of it and confess it, but only until you have made from your heart, when you pray, at least an act of the love of God and of contrition. That finally, if you were even not to make an act of love or of contrition, yet it would be pardoned the first time you go to Confession; for sound theology teaches that in Confession are pardoned not only the sins we confess (even though our sorrow for sin be from the universal motive only, that is, for having deserved hell), but also all the other sins of which we are not aware, and on which we are silent merely by reason of ignorance, and not from the malicious desire to suppress them. See, then, how little apprehension you ought to feel about hidden mortal sins, the fear of which in your case is a mere spectral fear, with which the demon tries to terrify you, in order to rob your heart of its peace.

§ 7. *Nor from fear that we may not have well repented of the sins of our past life.*

But I understand very well that you are not yet satisfied—not yet disposed to tranquillise yourself.

You will say to me, 'I am dreadfully afraid that I have not yet sufficiently repented of the sins of my past life, and therefore I cannot feel assured that God has pardoned me.' Very well: now tell me—what reason have you to doubt that you have not sufficiently repented? If you will reflect a little concerning yourself, you will see that you have every possible reason for judging that your repentance has been a true and sincere one. Is it not true that if, in your past life, you committed mortal sins, you have amended your ways, and do not fall into them now? Is it not true that your life is different now from what it was then? Is it not true that while you then committed mortal sins, because you could not bear to mortify your passions, you would not commit such sins now, were it to save you from suffering death? Well, then, this proves that you have every security that God has given you the grace of a true repentance, and that your will, however much it may formerly have been attached to sin, is now just as much alienated from it. In fact, without the grace of a true repentance, without this change in your will, how could you have been able to abandon these sins and amend your life? How could you have the resolution to suffer any evil whatever rather than offend God?

You see that this apprehension also is vain. Of the sins of your past life be always penitent, because by this means you will always secure yourself most effectually from falling back into them; but meanwhile be peaceful and tranquil, feeling that these ancient stains are wiped away, and that your soul is fully purified in the Blood of our Redeemer.

Ah, how truly unhappy is the life of this world! Those who are living in mortal sin for months and years, without the least thought or intention of seeking to be at peace with God, have no fears at all; while those, on the other hand, who love our Lord sincerely, and ought in consequence to be peaceful and tranquil, allow themselves often to be overpowered by tormenting anxieties. Those souls are indeed deserving of compassion who, although so well disposed that they would not only sacrifice everything sooner than commit a mortal sin, but even sooner than commit a venial sin of which they were fully aware, are nevertheless always in anguish, and scarcely have a moment's peace, from the dread lest they should be in disfavour with God. How can it be possible for your house to be infested with hawks and jackdaws if you take pains to drive away everything, down to a little fly? Banish, then, these fears; nay, if you do not know that you are guilty of hidden and positive mortal sins of which you have not repented, set aside these terrors—despise them, once for all, as coming from the demon, who is endeavouring to convulse and disorder the depths of your heart. And I say *positive mortal* sins, because doubtful mortal sins in you, who fear God, are only scruples, as your spiritual director must already have taught you, to whom you should refer and be obedient, as I have told you in the fifth and last chapter.

Pardon me now a little prolixity if I cannot yet conclude, having arrived at this most important point of endeavouring to persuade souls too timorous before God that they should live in a quiet assurance of the Divine friendship, and pluck away out of their hearts the doubt, as malignant as it is disquieting, that they may be in some way or other stained by the guilt of mortal sin. It is a point of the utmost importance, because this doubt hinders the outpourings of love, chills good works, extinguishes our longing after the joys of paradise, and throws us back again into a love of this life. How, indeed, could my heart take flight towards God in vivid and ardent flames of affection, if it were inwardly wounded by a doubt which might thus be put into words?—'I indeed give vent to my feelings in these acts of love, but perhaps they are after all only deceptive. Instead of having in my heart really and truly that holy charity which I thus flaunt before Almighty God, I may be possibly stained with the guilt of mortal sin.' Should I not then feel my heart griped, as it were, by a hand of ice, and should I not fall into consternation? And when endeavouring to occupy myself in works of religion, of zeal, of charity, should I not be chilled and unmanned by the reflection that possibly, my soul being deprived of sanctifying grace, all these good works are dead before God, since none can bear heavenly fruits of merit? And how could I desire the end of this life of misery and sin, and long for eternal blessedness? 'Ah,' I should say to myself, 'although I am not aware of having committed some dreadful sins which hinder my eternal salvation, nevertheless I may perhaps be stained with them; and when I die, believing that I am about to be united to God, my only Good, I may instead be precipitated into the arms of Satan, my eternal enemy! Surely it is better to live on in this world than to desire to leave it—a step fraught with such tremendous peril!' Ah, timorous soul, abhor sin beyond every other evil, for certainly all sin deserves an eternal, infinite abhorrence; but do not therefore try with disquieting doubts to suffocate the voice, which is that of the Holy Spirit, dwelling by the mercy of God in your hearts, and which assures you that you are children of God: 'Ipse enim Spiritus testimonium reddit spiritui nostro quod sumus filii Dei' (Rom. viii. 16), —' For the Spirit Himself giveth testimony to our spirit that we are the sons of God.' From the sure confidence which this voice will inspire there will come upon you that interior joy—that joy of the Lord which forms your true strength: 'Gaudium etenim Domini est fortitudo nostra,'—' For the joy of the Lord is our strength' (2 Esd. viii. 10). There are some who would keep souls in a perpetual state of anxiety, in the most agonising state of doubt, under pretence of keeping them in a state of humility; but we say of such persons *ignorant et errant*—they are ignorant and in error— because they are unable to distinguish that which is conducive to true humility from that which conduces to distrust, and sometimes even to despair. That very learned theologian, Scavini, did not hesitate to teach that the repentant sinner may feel as certain that his sins are pardoned as he feels certain of having committed them (*De Sac. Pœnit. de Absol. vir. et eff.*, edit. 1ª).

§ 8. *Nor ought one to lose confidence from the fear of having consented to wicked thoughts.*

Souls that fear God have so great an abhorrence of sin that, when they are tempted, the mere possibility of committing sin throws them at times into such a state of agitation, and hence into such apprehension of having committed it, that they are seized with an overwhelming terror of being lost; and if they cannot have palpable proofs of having resisted the temptation, they cannot find any peace. In one respect, happy are these souls that have such a tender love of God! If the mere possibility of sinning makes them tremble, they are very far indeed from falling into it. But, on the other hand, their excessive fears are unreasonable, do not please God, and in many ways may hinder their spiritual advancement. While they are desiring palpable proofs of not having consented to temptation, they are easily tranquillised with regard to outward sins, because, not having committed the evil deed which they know they might have committed, they feel assured that they resisted the tempter. But when it is a question of internal sins they are deprived of all arguments of this kind, and consequently suffer tortures of irremediable anguish. The soul, frightened by the temptation of an evil thought, no sooner feels the impression of it than she begins to fear that she has not combated it as it was her duty to do. Then to this fear succeeds another that she may have consented; and then comes the torturing suspicion of having fallen into mortal sin and forfeited the friendship of God. Then the soul begins to dispute with conscience in the most searching and subtle manner. At one moment she seems to remember having resisted the evil thought, at another she is confronted by a terrible suspicion of having consented. The longer the self-colloquy lasts the greater is the internal confusion; and thus the poor soul is bereft of all peace. In the mean time the imagination retraces all over again the appearances and the impressions of the temptation; hence new doubts and new tortures are quickly reproduced, and the more the soul feels tempted the more she believes herself to be wicked in the sight of God, and inclined to sin, until at length she judges it to be impossible that, assailed by so many temptations, she has not been overcome by at least one. Then she feels persuaded of having sinned. Not even the authority of the confessor can remove this impression. If he imposes on such penitents the obligation of calming these fears, and assures them that they were not in fault, then they come to the conclusion that they have not explained their case properly—that the confessor did not sufficiently understand them—and their anguish and agitation only increase. O devout soul who read this little book, do you in the least degree resemble the picture I have drawn? If so, for the love of God calm yourself for a moment and listen to me. You suspect—or perhaps you are even convinced—that you fall frequently into sins of thought, either against faith or against charity to your neighbour, and perhaps more often still against chastity. O poor soul, I pity you if you sin habitually against this most precious virtue! But tell me, do you frequently sin *outwardly* in word and in action against these virtues? Do you put forth heretical opinions? Do you ever calumniate your neighbour? Do you commit offences against holy chastity? You answer me that, by the grace of God, you are not accustomed to fall into these outward sins, and I too am convinced of this fact, without your telling me; for otherwise I know that you would not be so fearful of offending Almighty God. Very well, then; if by the grace of God you do not fall into these external sins, you ought to feel sure that you do not commit those inward sins which keep you in such a state of apprehension. If the fear of God suffices to restrain your passions in such manner that you do not satisfy them by committing sin, very much more will it restrain you from committing sins of thought. You would indeed be a strange sort of being if your malicious love of sinning in your thoughts were so strong and continuous, while it was quite the reverse as regards sins of deed. Could it ever be possible that a person having the power to eat flesh-meat on Friday should never do so, and yet continually take pleasure in wishing for it, and in fancying that he was always eating it on those forbidden days? Ah! the malice of our evil nature finds much more satisfaction in committing sin than in picturing sin to the imagination. Do you abstain from evil deeds where your passions would find the greater gratification? This of itself is a decisive argument that you do not consent to evil thoughts. But your excessive fear produces such a state of confusion in your soul that you mistake temptation for consent, although between the one and the other there is the same difference as there is between seeing the poison in a glass bottle and swallowing it. Does there seem to you any difference in these two things? Well, then, there is precisely the same difference between temptation to sin and your consent thereto. Temptation of itself, as such, has never injured any soul, even as the poison, while it remains shut up in the vial, injures nobody. In order to sin, the consent of the will is necessary, and in order to sin mortally we must give our full and deliberate consent to something that is gravely prohibited by the law of God. Be satisfied and tranquil. If you abstain from evil deeds you may feel certain that you do not willingly or wilfully commit sins of thought, even though a hundred—a thousand doubts should arise in your heart.

You will answer perhaps that one may sin more easily in thought, that less time is necessary for sins of thought than for those of action; that hence it is easier to fall into internal than external sins. Quite so; but how much time would it take you to say that 'there is no God'? How much time would it take to commit an unworthy action? Yet you neither do nor say the one nor the other. Besides, if your will is so evil as to renounce the grace of God, as seriously and knowingly to blaspheme our Lord, does it not take as much determination to commit a sin of some duration as to commit one of a single minute? Besides, in a momentary sin the evil will has but little satisfaction, while in a sin of longer duration the satisfaction is much greater. And, in fact, one sees that those people who have abandoned themselves to iniquity not only commit outward sins of action which last some space of time, but when they consent to evil thoughts, either from complacency or from desire, instead of harbouring them for one single moment, as you are afraid of doing, they entertain them for whole hours together, until the imagination becomes wearied. Besides all this, the greater number of those internal sins which cause you such anguish are sins of complacency; consequently, if the soul finds no complacency in such and such malicious or evil thoughts, it has not sinned; and how can you, with any show of reason, fear that you yield with complacency to thoughts which are so wearisome to you, which you fear so much, which you so greatly abhor? And do you not see that complacency and abhorrence, with regard to one and the same object, is in itself a contradiction? A passionate lover of wine—a drunkard, so long as he is such, cannot abhor wine; and if he begins to abhor it he ceases to be a passionate lover of it, and is no longer a drunkard.

But let us have done with this once for all. When your spiritual director assures you that you should not be afraid of your evil thoughts, since, however much they may trouble you, you are not losing the grace of God—believe him out of compassion to yourself, believe him for the love of God. I pray you most earnestly by the precious wounds of our Saviour to do so, knowing as I do the anguish which your fears cause you, and the impediments which they are to your spiritual advancement.

Do you know when you ought really to have scruples, and accuse yourself of your evil thoughts? (I am speaking to those who have been commanded by their confessors not to be troubled on account of them.) Only when you are so positively certain that you voluntarily and with full deliberation consented to them, that you could take a solemn oath to this effect on the holy Gospels, or on the Cross of Christ. If you are not so certain of it that you could freely take such an oath, then you should take no account of such thoughts; and of this you are assured by the holy Bishop St. Alphonsus Liguori and a thousand other theologians. Now tell me, could you freely take an oath on the holy Gospels or on the Cross of Christ that you gave full and deliberate consent to these evil thoughts which continually disquiet you and destroy your peace? I should like to see if you could have the

THE HOLY FEAR OF GOD. 147

courage to take such an oath. 'But suppose I have not thoroughly explained myself—suppose my confessor did not fully understand me.' Even if your confessor did not entirely understand you—and take note that this fear is one of your follies, because God has promised to illuminate confessors, so that they may thoroughly understand their penitents — however badly you may have expressed yourself, provided you have not wilfully deceived your confessor—in short whatever he or you may have done in the matter, St. Alphonsus and a thousand theologians will tell you that you must obey, and be silent, and be tranquil, if you are not sufficiently sure to be able to take the oaths I have mentioned. Now do you think that you alone know more about these things than a thousand theologians, together with St. Alphonsus, of whom the Church has pronounced that in his works there is nothing open to censure?

You must know furthermore that this saint, supported by the arguments and authority of other theologians, considering the anxiety of mind you feel about consenting to evil thoughts only results in multiplying them, and that frequently for a long time you have fought against them,—this great saint tells you that you are not even obliged positively to chase away these evil thoughts, but on the contrary, may let them come and go as they list, merely taking care not voluntarily to feel pleasure in them. And this you may do with tranquillity, even though these evil thoughts cause you those sufferings which torment you, and make you feel so ashamed. Humble yourself on account of these annoyances, but do not pay attention to them. If they torment you it is a sign that they do not give you pleasure, and that is enough to satisfy you that you are not in fault. At any rate, therefore, you ought to maintain your tranquillity; you ought to feel sure of being in the grace of God; of enjoying the Divine friendship, and so keep peace in your heart.

'But I am in constant fear of offending God. I am afraid of doing wrong in everything, whether I think or act; yet I go on thinking and acting. Now if I continue to act and think with this perpetual fear upon me, without laying it aside, without clearing my conscience, without feeling sure that I am doing what is right, shall I not sin?'

This is one of the most subtle deceits of the demon, by which he keeps souls in a state of agitation; but St. Alphonsus replies to this difficulty also (*Tract. de Cons.* n. 19), and teaches that you

THE HOLY FEAR OF GOD. 149

are under the obligation of despising this fear—that you should not seek to feel sure in your conscience of being right, but that you should act and think as if this fear had no existence. Consequently you should take no notice of the things you have done and thought with this fear upon you, and still less should you confess them. In short, be persuaded that you should not seek to tranquillise yourself by the force of reasoning; for you will only be able to accomplish it by the power of holy obedience—and will you ever regret having done so? 'An obedient soul is never lost,' say the Saints, and you need not fear that you will be the first.

§ 9. *Neither should the continual danger of falling into mortal sin cause us to lose our tranquillity of heart.*

One great fear which frequently causes much anguish to some devout souls is the possibility, from one moment to another, of falling into mortal sin, particularly when suffering from great and continual temptations. 'What use is it,' a man may say to himself, 'that I may be in the grace of God now? In a moment I may lose it, as sometimes even great saints have done; consequently I might at any minute fall into hell, as I should deserve to do, by committing a mortal sin. And how easily, tempted as I am, might such a calamity happen to me!' But neither should this thought deprive you of peace. Do you imagine that one falls into mortal sin, and thence into hell, by a misfortune, as travellers walking in the dark fall into the ditches that are by the wayside? In order to fall into mortal sin one must first have the evil will to do so. But you, up to the present time, have not this evil will—you have not this desire to sin; and therefore until you have it you cannot sin mortally. You will, however, answer me, that you may have this evil will at any moment, and hence at any moment fall into mortal sin. This is perfectly true; yet although we cannot doubt that even a moment of time would suffice for a soul that fears God to yield to a temptation, and sin mortally, ought one on this account to live continually in dread of this peril? Is it not true that you, a son, may lose in one moment the love that you bear to your father, that this love might all be changed to hate? Is it not true that you, a sister, may in one moment turn into dislike the affection which you have hitherto felt for your sister? All this is quite true. But the fact that these and suchlike things are possible does not make them happen, and no person that loves another would ever afflict and torment himself about the possibility of some day or other changing his affection into hatred. If you answer me that you find yourself drawn to consent to these temptations, I answer you that you have the grace of God to support you, in order that the power of the temptation may not drag you down into the abyss. And He will support you with His grace—that God who is the great lover of souls,—'qui amas animas' (Wisd. xi. 27). Together with His grace the love that you bear to Him will support you, through which love you feel that you would rather die than offend Him; and the fear which you rightly have of hell supports you also—that hell which you would deserve by committing mortal sin; and you are moreover shielded by the hideousness of sin, which always inspires horror in the soul that fears God, a horror which is so much the greater when the temptation comes near at hand; and the most Holy Mary supports you, in whose succour you confide; and your angel guardian sustains you, who knows more how to make all things work together for your good than the demon knows how to make them tend to your disadvantage. And do you think that it is an easy task for the demon to endeavour to despoil of sanctifying grace a soul that fears God, and induce her to fall into mortal sin, even though one moment of full and deliberate consent is sufficient to make her guilty? The fortress is taken in one moment, for it falls either when the enemy enters the gates that he has first beaten down, or passes through the breach he has opened; but often, before that moment comes, many weeks and many months pass by; and if the fortress is well manned, well armed, and well provided, that moment never arrives; so that the enemy, wearied and laughed to scorn, is forced to retire. But you will say, 'Even the saints sometimes have fallen, notwithstanding that they had all the helps you have named. How much more easily, then, shall I fall!' I must tell you, however, that those real saints who have fallen are much fewer perhaps than you imagine.* Indeed without speaking of great saints, but only of those souls that live quite determined to avoid sin, and endeavour to give themselves wholly to God, directors of conscience find from practical experience that such are not wont to incur the misfortune of falling into mortal sin. Moreover it is a

---

* 'They are not many, but very few, who, after lives admirable for sanctity and penitence, are yet condemned.' *Tresors de Conf.* p. ii. c. vii. dif. 3.

THE HOLY FEAR OF GOD.   153

comfort to know that many never committed mortal sin, and that a still greater number who formerly used to fall into mortal sins never after their conversion, during a period of many, very many years, committed them again.

Oh, do not think that all the world is going to destruction. The grace of our Saviour works admirably in a great number of souls, and indeed in all those who humbly correspond with it. A great number of souls who, together with the saints already in heaven, will form that great multitude— of whom St. John the Evangelist, who saw them, says, that no man could number them: 'turbam magnam quam dinumerare nemo poterat' (Ap. vii. 39),—'a great multitude which no man could number.' Certain persons there are in the world who, overcome by grief at seeing all the evil which in fact is done, and the great numbers of people who appear to live only to offend God,—such persons allow themselves to be seized with a melancholy which makes them look crookedly at all things, as the holy Prophet Elias did one day when he thought that he was the only true worshipper of God remaining in Israel. Do not allow yourself to be overtaken by this melancholy idea, which is good for nothing but to oppress the heart, and make you give vent to useless lamentations. In the world, it is true, there are many wicked people, and these are also more numerous than the good. But of the good there are also a great number, a most consoling number, who are the delight of our Lord, and form the triumph of His victorious grace. How many souls there are who live always in the grace of God, and never fall into mortal sin! Among this number you may be, provided that you desire it. But certainly you do desire it; and your anxiety not to lose grace assures me that you desire it. Have firm confidence, then, and do not torment yourself with fears on account of the temptations which assail you so strongly and so frequently. It is clear that God permits them in order to be able to crown you with a particular glory in Heaven. One cannot have great victories without great combats; and great victors receive great crowns. The saints love most the souls that are most tempted, and hope from them great things. 'But,' you will reply perhaps, 'I dread bieng conquered and falling at one time or another.' Have firm confidence that you will not fall, and I too have a firm confidence for you that our Lord, did He foresee that you were on the point of falling, would make you die sooner than allow you to fall from Him. He knows that you would rather die than offend Him, and do you imagine that He will not give you at the very least the grace to die sooner than offend Him grievously? Say to our Lord: 'I have no fear in this world but that of offending Thee, O my God, and becoming Thine enemy. If Thou foreseest that, by continuing to live, this tremendous calamity will fall upon me, let me die, I beseech Thee, instead. Death, which is the evil of all evils the most abhorred by the world, will be for me the greatest grace, the greatest blessing.' You may then rest secure in the goodness of God.

'But,' you say, 'the saints who have fallen cause me too great a terror.' The saints who have fallen, I answer, ought to be no cause of terror to you; the recollection should rather melt your heart with humility, because those saints who have fallen (as St. Alphonsus observes, *Pract. of the Love of Jesus Christ*, c. x.) have fallen precisely because they first allowed themselves to come under the dominion of pride. They gloried in themselves, and hence were ruined miserably. Therefore let the memory of these saints keep you firmly fixed and rooted in humility, but do not be terrified; for humility is advantageous in all things, terror is of no use whatever. Humble yourself continually and profoundly before God, for this will put you in an infallible state of security. So do not be disconcerted because you feel yourself tempted, even greatly tempted, by pride; for if the demon of pride is knocking continually at the door of your heart it is a proof that he has not yet entered therein. Pray—be tranquil, for God will not permit him to enter.

Finally, you should aspire to that bold confidence in God which made St. Paul say: 'I am sure that neither death, nor life, nor angels, nor principalities, nor powers,* nor things present, nor things to come, nor might, nor height, nor depth, nor any other creature can separate us from the love of God which is in Jesus Christ our Lord' (Rom. viii. 38, 39). A hope so secure, so solid, rooted in God alone, from whom comes all our strength and sufficiency, will be the most efficient means of not falling any more; and it will be so for two reasons. In the first place, because the merit of hope is great, and the firmer and more perfect the hope is, the greater is the merit. Meanwhile this merit disposes us for the reception of Divine grace; and the greater our merit is, the better we are disposed to receive

* The angels, principalities, and powers of darkness—that is, the demons. See Corn. à Lap.

grace abundantly, so that the aids to grace being multiplied, our perseverance is made daily more and more certain on the part of God. Secondly, the assurance that we are obtaining a great good, a supreme good (which constant perseverance in friendship with God certainly is), gives us great courage to overcome every difficulty, every obstacle which comes in the way of our progress ; and then no means are neglected by us, however arduous and severe, provided they may prove efficacious. Hence our ever-increasing coöperation is united to the increase of the grace of God, and perseverance is thus daily more and more assured even by our own act.

§ 10. *The holy fear of God ought to inspire great confidence.*

Wherefore does our Lord inspire in us the sentiments of His holy fear ? Tell me for what end does He bestow on us this grace, namely, that we should fear His judgments and His chastisements ? Have you ever reflected on this ? The answer is soon found. He inspires in us the feeling of His holy fear that we may avoid sin, that we may repent when we have sinned, that we may not fall under the weight of His severe judgments, that we may go free from the chastisements of sin; in a word, He desires that we may fear Him, in order that He may not be forced to chastise us. Therefore He inspires in us the sentiments of His holy fear, not to make us experience the terrible effects of His justice, but the gentle and loving force of His mercy. If the case be so then, as it most certainly is, does it not appear very clearly evident that this same fear of God ought to inspire the greatest confidence in us? and that this confidence should not merely be felt by the just, but also by sinners, even by those most laden with iniquities? To feel a holy fear of God is to have a pledge, an earnest, of the mercy which He desires to bestow upon us. If, by reason of our sins, He did not mean to show us pity any longer, neither would He give us the grace of fearing Him, because this grace is always given for the end that we may obtain His pardon. When therefore you feel within yourself that you have the fear of God, of His judgments, of His chastisements, these very emotions ought to make you feel sure that God is reserving for you, not the rigours of His justice, but the loving proofs of His mercy.*

* Hear with what force St. Bernard expresses this truth: 'Ipse timor firmissima quædam est et efficax materia spei, siquidem maximum quoddam Dei donum est timor iste, et ex percep-

And suppose that, instead of being a pious and devout soul, you were a sinner, guilty of many crimes, feeling your heart shaken by the fear of death, of judgment, of hell—even then your heart should immediately be enlarged and strengthened by a feeling of great confidence. And I say a great confidence, because our confidence should always exceed our fear. What! Is not Almighty God more good and more merciful than we are bad? and while the voice of our sins cries out for vengeance and chastisement, does not the voice of the Blood of our Lord Jesus Christ cry out infinitely more for peace and pardon? Yes, we should confide much more in the benignity of God than we should fear His justice, because, after all, the only thing which can properly cause us to fear is the malice of our own guilt, which, however great it may be, is not infinite; and, on the other hand, our hope should be in the merits of our Lord Jesus Christ, which are truly of infinite value. Therefore we should exercise ourselves much more in sentiments

---

tione præsentium firma est expectatio futurorum' (St. Ber. apud Scavini, *de Spei cert.* art. 1),—' This fear is itself a most secure and efficacious source of hope, since fear is one of the greatest of God's gifts, and from the realisation of things present there springs a most lively hope of things to come.'

of hope than in those of fear. In fact, if you are one of those who are able to do so, read the Holy Scriptures from beginning to end; then, if you can, read all the public prayers of the Church, and you will see that for every hundred sentences which inspire you with confidence in the Divine goodness you will perhaps find but one which speaks of the terrors of God's justice. This is undoubtedly a valid argument to make us know how much God desires us to have confidence rather than fear.

But in conclusion tell me, what is it that you most desire on earth? Is it not true that you desire to be good in the sight of God, to be pleasing in His most pure eyes? If an angel were to reveal to you that God is satisfied with you, and were to assure you that God has a satisfaction in you as in a soul which is His delight, would you not be satisfied, would you not consider yourself to be completely happy? Yes, it is so—you cannot deny it; your one great desire is to be good in the sight of God. Now then imagine a daughter, who has many defects which disgust her father, even as you are laden with sins which are hateful to God, and that she desires nothing so much as to become good, that she may content her father and be pleasing in his eyes; suppose moreover that it is in her father's power to change her heart and make her good whenever he chooses, and that consequently his daughter presents herself to him and says, kneeling at his feet: 'Dear father, you see how wicked I am, how often I do things which are hateful to you, and bitter to your heart. What grieves me the most is that I should displease and grieve you. You can change my heart, you can give me a good instead of an evil will, and change me into a respectful, obedient, loving daughter, who shall content you in everything, as it is now my one desire to do. Dear father, I ask of you no other grace than this—to change my heart and my will in such a manner that from henceforth you may be truly satisfied with me. If you see that in order to change my heart and my will it is necessary to give me some chastisement, chastise me then, I beseech you, as you may think best for me. In all things I am willing to submit, if you will only grant me that I may never displease you any more, but in all things content you.'

Suppose such a daughter speaking thus to such a father, would it be possible for the father to resist such an entreaty, and not grant such a favour? You can see very well that it would be impossible; the heart of the father would be melted with tenderness, and the daughter's request would certainly be granted. She would certainly not fail to have the consolation of seeing herself become good and pleasing in all things to her father. But in this world there is no father who has power to change the hearts of his children. This Father we have in Heaven. Yes, O devout, but perhaps too diffident and timorous soul, this Father you possess in Heaven. Repeat to Him, word for word, the prayer of that humble daughter, and do not fancy that He can have a heart hard enough to refuse you. And that you may render yourself still more sure, ask your great Mother, whom you have also in Heaven, to intercede for you, so that you obtain this same grace—your great Mother Mary, who has such power with God, your Heavenly Father, and is so much beloved by Him that not all the hosts of Heaven put together are so near to His heart or so beloved by Him as she is. Therefore peacefully, in tranquillity, and in security, HAVE CONFIDENCE IN GOD.

CONCLUSION OF THE APPENDIX.

CAN you imagine how important it is that your fear of God should have the above-mentioned conditions—so that it should never be severed from peace and tranquillity, but be full of confidence in Him? Happy are you if you perfectly understand this. You will make rapid and sure progress on the path of Christian perfection, because you will be able to avoid stepping into those pitfalls which the demon prepares for pious souls. This master of all deception sees all those who walk along the way of this mortal life, divided, as it were, into two great troops. Some, under the banner of the world, pass along puffed up and presuming on their own strength and power, despising the gravest perils, and hastening towards the precipitous termination of the slippery road that leads to perdition; others, on the contrary, following the Cross of our Redeemer, humble and diffident of themselves, walk cautiously and carefully, that they may not mistake the way of salvation. Those who are going along that miserable road, and are so near being precipitated into the hidden abyss, should be made to feel a salutary terror, in order that they may discontinue their fatal onward course, and not persist in their foolish imaginings; the others, on the contrary, who are struggling along the right way, and go on ascending gradually the steep but safe mountain of salvation, ought to be encouraged and refreshed, that they may not be weary of persevering in it. But the malignant demon, on the contrary, applauds and spurs on the unhappy ones, who are rushing headlong to destruction, until they fall suddenly and unexpectedly into the yawning gulf of eternal death, while he endeavours to terrify and discourage those who are on the right road, so that they may stop or turn back, instead of going on securely, and ascending cautiously to the possession of eternal life. Malignant demon! He shows such skill that it often happens that neither the one set of people nor the other—neither the good nor the bad—are aware of his deceits. Those who ought to tremble exceedingly, because they are enemies of God and obstinate in sin, he excites to presumption, while he attempts to discourage those who ought to be full of hope, as being friends of God and persevering in the practice of Christian virtue. Can it be possible that a deception so great, so clear moreover and manifest, should not be recognised by every one? Oh, take care that you do recognise it, and that you render vain and useless, once for all, these arts of your great enemy.

If you will put out of your head the needless solicitudes, fears, and anxieties which disturb it continually, and will walk boldly on the road of Christian perfection, this is what you will gain :—

First, you will feel the sweeness of serving God; you will have the consolations of Divine grace, through which you will become more and more firm and constant in His service, and with which you will more readily and easily correspond. David not only walked, but says, 'I have run on the way of Thy commandments, after Thou hast strengthened mine heart.'

Secondly, you will frequent with greater assiduity the most holy Sacraments, and, above all, the most august Sacrament of the Eucharist; and instead of obliging your director to give you positive commands to overcome your fears, you will ask of him permission to communicate frequently, to be nourished by this most sustaining food of the soul, from which, though it is not wrong to abstain sometimes through humility, it is always right not to abstain through love.*

* I mean, of course, when your director advises it.

Thirdly, you will live more detached from this miserable world, because the secure hope of obtaining Paradise will enable you to regard death with a tranquil eye, knowing that it will set you free from so much unhappiness, and put you in possession of a never-ending beatitude.

Fourthly, you will make virtue appear more lovable to others, and will draw them more easily to practise it, because your maxims will have in them nothing that is rigorous and bitter. They will be the gentle maxims of the Gospel, which, when they are not misunderstood or misrepresented, so sweetly attract the hearts of others. Those who are now tossed about by the tempest of their unbridled passions, will see the calm of your spirit, and will also desire to experience this holy calm, renouncing their own inordinate desires. Oh, what harm is done to piety by those pious souls that are always agitated by fears, always cramped by anxieties! Worldlings, seeing this, congratulate themselves that they are worldly, imagining that without anxiety, agitation, and a troubled spirit there cannot be true piety.

Fifthly, you will have and will cultivate zeal for the salvation of souls according to your capacity, in whatever state or condition you may be;

for souls that are free from agitation, anxiety, and fear hasten unshackled along the heavenly road, not content merely with insuring their own salvation, but occupied with the endeavour to save others, finding an ineffable delight in leading souls to God. But souls that are agitated by importunate fears, souls that are continually wanting to feel secure, and are continually falling into greater uncertainty, have neither time nor inclination to think of the good of others ; hence they fall into a certain spiritual egotism, which makes them almost forget the salvation of souls; nay, by imagining perils and difficulties in everything, they think that they could not give their mind to the salvation of others without neglecting their own. Oh, how many there are who would have time and capacity to coöperate in this Divine, this most Divine labour, as St. Dionysius calls it, the salvation of souls ! And how and on what are their time and their capacity wasted ? In tormenting themselves by examinations of conscience which never end, in the apprehension of sins which they never committed, in terror, in fearing chastisements which they never have merited, or which, if indeed they have merited such, they ought no longer to fear, because they ought to feel confident of having obtained pardon.

Ah, do not be among the number of these! Rise above this state of misery, if indeed you are lying in it! Do you not see how much good you may do to the souls of others redeemed by the same precious Blood that redeemed you? You may correct sinners, you may admonish the erring, you may direct and counsel the doubting, you may confirm the weak, you may infuse fervour into the lukewarm; and if you cannot, and know not how to do anything else, you can pray for all. Yes, you can pray; and offer Masses and Communions for the conversion of sinners and infidels,—that every soul may be turned to God, and find in Him life and salvation. But how can you have zeal sufficient to accomplish all you might do, if your heart be not peaceful, tranquil, and full of confidence in God?

Courage! then; and 'may the peace of God, which surpasseth all understanding, keep your hearts and minds in Christ Jesus' (Philip. iv. 7). 'Let the peace of Christ rejoice in your hearts' (Col. iii. 15). 'Rejoice in the Lord always: again, I say, rejoice' (Philip. iv. 4). 'Serve ye the Lord with gladness' (Ps. xcix. 1). Oh, how much good you will gain from the peace, from the spiritual joy o your heart! No, you can neither know nor imagine it until you experience it. Seek it, then, from Almighty God continually for yourself and for all devout souls, and, fortifying yourself with the intercession of our Blessed Lady, be not weary of repeating,

'Causa nostræ lætitiæ, ora pro nobis.'

NOTES.

Note 1. (See page 44.)

DUPLICITUR in eis (passionibus) potest malum inveniri uno modo ex ipsa specie passionis. . . . . Sicut invidia secundum suam speciem importat quoddam malum . . . . et ideo vindicta mox nominata sonat aliquid mali. . . . . Hoc autem non competit iræ quæ est appetitus vindictæ, potest enim vindicta et bene et mali appeti.

Alio modo invenitur malum in aliqua passione secundum quantitatem ipsius; et sic potest malum in ira inveniri, quando scilicet aliquis irascitur plus vel minus præter rationem rectam, si autem quis irascitur secundum rationem rectam, tunc irasci est laudabile.

Hæc autem ira etsi in ipsa executione actus judicium rationis aliqualiter impediat; non tamen rectitudinem rationis tollit. . . . Non est autem contra rationem virtutis, ut intermittatur deliberatio rationis in executione eius, quod est a ratione deliberatum (S. Thom. 2—2, q. 158, a. 1). Ira fuit in Christo . . . . ira quæ transgreditur ordinem rationis opponitur mansuetudini, non autem ira quæ est moderata et ad medium reducta per rationem (p. iii. q. 15, a. 9).

Note 2. *On the necessity of moderation in explaining maxims that strike terror.* (See page 126, § 3.)

I would here make known, as well to preachers as to writers of ascetic books, a certain desire of mine,

which is, that in treating of what is terrible in the
truths of our holy Faith, which certainly should
neither be concealed nor explained away, they should
always show some consideration for those timid and
too apprehensive souls that come in such large numbers to hear sermons and instructions, and who,
oftener than others, read and meditate on writings of
that kind. Some people, when they speak or write
of judgment, hell, &c., seem as if they had no other
object but that of frightening people. We see in them
a constant effort to seek out arguments that will strike
terror into the mind, and images that will make the
most vivid impression possible on the fancy. They
drive hearers and readers into a state of consternation, and there leave them, believing themselves to
have achieved the greatest amount of success when
they have succeeded in producing the greatest amount
of fear. Now I admit that this method may prove
useful in the case of obstinate and unimpressionable
sinners, to rouse them a little out of their lethargy ; but
we must also have some consideration for souls that
are delicately conscientious and over-sensitive. These
derive no benefit from such terrors, but, on the contrary, a great deal of harm. Their peace of mind is
lost, their confidence in our Lord weakened.

I would that in the administration of the Divine
word, no less than in the works of ascetical writers,
those truths of our holy Faith were explained with
the force and simplicity of the Divine Scriptures, without any of those subtleties and strainings of the imagination which the holy Fathers, I think, never made
use of when announcing them, orally or in writing, to
the people.

These latter times have produced certain sermons

and certain meditations on the eternal maxims, so constructed for the purpose of engendering horrors and extreme fear in the mind that no similar treatment of the subject could be met with in the whole Library of the Fathers. And yet they also had a vivid imagination, a lively faith and force of expression, so that they could have done at least as much. If they kept themselves within more moderate bounds, it was because they esteemed such moderation to be more suitable and more useful.

I could never wish that the sacred orator or the ascetic writer should deliberately aim at striking terror into souls, but rather that he should try to move them in a salutary manner, and make them turn to our Lord with strong but quiet feelings, that will not cause confusion and disturbance in the imagination. I wish indeed that they would never mention the terrible maxims without bringing in some hopeful one at the end; for this is of the utmost necessity, in order that the sinner, once aroused, may resolve to change his manner of life. The sinner who is only frightened will be more disposed to despair than to be converted; and that is why I cannot believe the method to be useful even for the most obstinate and unimpressionable sinners, since either they will not be moved at all by those terrors, or, if they are, they will feel an injurious kind of consternation rather than a salutary repentance. I am the more confirmed in this opinion by having observed that, in the arguments put forth by those preachers and ascetic writers who are most ardent in their zeal for the salvation of souls, fear is always tempered with hope. St. Gregory the Great, addressing himself to preachers (*Morals*, book xxxiii. chap. xi.), expressly inculcates the principle. He says:

'The preacher who has to instruct sinners should do so with such prudence that he will neither deprive them of fear and leave them nothing but hope, nor deprive them of hope and leave them nothing but fear.'

When I say this, however, I do not in the least mean to approve of those sacred orators of the present day who would accommodate the Divine word to the taste of the age, and by such a manner of expounding take from the eternal maxims their force, their vigour, and even the savour of the Faith, besmearing and disguising them with a cold and most empty philosophy. But in saying that I wished they would imitate the holy Fathers I have expressed my sentiments clearly enough.

If we *must* fall into some excess in speaking to sinners, let it be in giving confidence and courage rather than helpless terror and dread. It will be the lesser evil of the two. For there is no doubt that it is a lesser evil to bring a soul into danger of presumption than to bring it into danger of despair.

By presumption Christians are deceived, and made to rush into perdition almost without being aware of it —those unhappy people hoping all the while to reach Heaven some day, though they never weary of labouring for hell, live a life' of iniquity, and in many cases are overtaken by death in that state, so that they perish miserably. However, there never was any one so stupidly presumptuous as to hope for eternal salvation without doing any good at all. Practically, presumption consists in hoping for Heaven without having the will to do what we must do if we are to go there, and in supposing that a few good works, quite insufficient of themselves for the purpose, ought almost to insure our eternal salvation. Hence there are to be found presumptuous people who hear the Holy Mass every day, who are assiduous, or at least not altogether negligent, in hearing the Divine word, who every day recite the Rosary and the usual prayers night and morning, who give alms and do other works of charity, and who approach the Holy Sacrament from time to time. It is true they are deceived; for all the while they are keeping to themselves other people's property, or continuing some sinful intercourse, or nourishing some hatred; or they have some other sinful habits of which they will not break themselves. They are deceived, wickedly presuming that after they have refused God's friendship during life their few good works will save them in death. Still they do these good works, and from good works one may always expect some good. While praying they may offer up a prayer to God from the heart which may obtain for them light and a salutary fear. While listening to the Divine word they may hear some maxim that will make a lively impression on their minds, and the same thing may happen if they fall in with an enlightened zealous confessor. So that there is always a foundation on which to rest hopes of their amendment; whence it follows that, though presumption is bad, it leaves a probability of salvation.

Despair, on the other hand, destroys the whole spiritual edifice from its foundations; so that when once a man is persuaded (horrible persuasion!) that for him there is no chance of mercy, there is no longer any resting-place for him; he looks upon God but as an enemy, and gives up all the means of salvation as being either useless or inopportune. Why should he pray? Why hear sermons and instructions? Why call to mind the eternal maxims? Why go near a confessor? Having once decided the point, that for him there is no longer a chance of salvation, how shall he hope that good works could be of any use to him? On the contrary, will it not seem to him more reasonable that he should altogether avoid thinking of his own soul, of God, of eternity, such thoughts being to him suggestive of nothing but misery and doom? Such a man has no longer anything to hope for, except in this world; so he unbridles every passion, and in the gratification of these—even the most brutal of them—he endeavours to quench his heart's unquenchable thirst for happiness. Hence his will becomes more and more perverse, his intellect more and more darkened; he easily falls into errors against the Faith, and would like to persuade himself that religion is a cheat, God a chimæra. Meanwhile, as the light of reason convinces him of the contrary, he feels himself drawn into a downright abhorrence of religion and hatred of God, so that it comes to this, that he no longer sins to gratify his own passions, but simply to insult God, which is nothing less than beginning in this world the diabolical life that will last eternally in hell.

These are not mere suppositions. They are facts which are repeated whenever a Christian gives himself up to the horrible sin of despair.

Thus the conclusion is forced upon us that presumption is a great evil, but despair the worst of evils, and infinitely more to be feared; and therefore we should be infinitely more afraid of excess in frightening souls than of excess in encouraging them.

NOTE 3. *How easy it is to make an act of the perfect love of God.* (See page 134.)

Some people have a deeply-rooted prejudice that it is very difficult to make a really perfect act of charity, and therefore of perfect contrition.

'It is all very well and easily said,' they tell us, 'to talk about making acts of the perfect love of God and acts of perfect contrition ; but how few there are, especially among the rougher sort, who really know how to do so from their hearts!' Those who think so had better become aware that they have fallen into a great error. All theologians agree that every Christian, from his first use of reason to the end of his life, is obliged, under pain of mortal sin, to make, from time to time, acts of the love of God, acts of the love of friendship, which is perfect love.

An excommunication was fulminated by Innocent II. (Prop. Condemn. sub 6) against those who assert that it is not of rigorous obligation to make an act of the love of God every five years; and many theologians, including St. Alphonsus, teach that this rigorous obligation is for every month (Lib. ii. No. 6 op. *Mor.*). Since, then, every Christian is obliged to make an act of the love of God frequently, shall we say that it is so very difficult to be able to do so—to know how to do so? Should we not be acting wrongly towards God, who gave us this precept, calling it the first and the greatest? Are not all the precepts of God's law such as to be easily fulfilled by those who have a good will, and are therefore assisted by His grace? Really it makes one laugh to hear people say that it is difficult for an uncultivated person to make an act of the perfect love of God! Do they suppose it to be a theological argument, requiring a groundwork of dialectics, and a knowledge of Scripture, of the Councils, and of the Fathers? Unhappy indeed would be the condition of rough and ignorant people, if the great precept of the love of God were more difficult for them than for the cultivated and the well taught. Is not an act of the love of God the noblest of the graces that the Saviour bestows? Has grace need of science and erudition in order to work within us? Does not grace of itself enlighten the intellect? Does it not of itself move the will? One must know very little indeed about the doctrine of Divine grace to tolerate a prejudice so unreasonable as this, that the love of God is more difficult for the uneducated than for the learned. How often, on the contrary, does science render its possessors puffed up and proud, and so impede the operations of grace, which works on the foundation of humility! How often do we find rough, uneducated people particularly well disposed to receive heavenly inspirations, because they offer to God a simple and humble heart! Do we not frequently meet with poor women and very rough countrymen who have a more ardent love of God than the most erudite doctors? You may see in St. Luke, chap. xi., that whilst the doctors of the law said of Christ, 'He casteth out devils by Beelzebub, the prince of devils,' the poor women exclaimed, 'Blessed is the womb that bore Thee, and the paps that gave Thee suck.' We therefore come to the conclusion that, by the help of Divine grace, it is as easy for all of us to make an act of the love of God, and therefore an act of contrition which is virtually included, as it is to do the other good works that every Christian must do.

Some people, indeed, find it difficult to make acts of the love of God or acts of contrition, because they suppose that they must arouse and form them by means of many considerations on the Divine Goodness. Such considerations are no doubt not only useful but, generally speaking, necessary when a person is in mortal sin, and therefore has lost the habit of the love of God; for his will is opposed to God, and he must use force to make it opposed to sin, and converted to God. But a soul that is in a state of grace does not require this force; for it possesses the habit of charity, and a habit is very easily reduced into action. Is it difficult for a blasphemer to blaspheme, or a thief to steal? Certainly not; for the one has the habit of stealing and the other of blaspheming. And so it is with the habit of the love of God—always supposing the assistance of grace, which God will not refuse. Observe, however, that even a person in mortal sin will not find it too difficult a thing to awaken the love of God in his heart by means of the before-mentioned considerations on the Divine Goodness; for the grace of God suggests these, and gently renders them efficacious.

NOTE 4. *On Zeal for the salvation of souls among secular persons.*

If to certain souls it should seem that none ought to aspire so high as this, except apostolic men whose office it is to be occupied with the spiritual health of their neighbours, they must pardon me if, instead of giving the short and direct reply that might be given, I answer indirectly with an example. They must pardon me, for it is so very edifying.

St. Mary Magdalene de' Pazzi had no apostolic mission; she was a virgin consecrated to peaceful contemplation within the walls of a convent. Yet it would be difficult to find any apostolic man who nourished in his heart a more ardent zeal for the salvation of souls. How sensitive she was about their interests—how affectionate! It seemed to her as nothing that she herself should love our Lord unless all the world loved Him. When she heard of the progress that our holy Faith was, at that time, making in India, she said that if, without prejudice to her vocation, she might travel the whole world for the purpose of saving souls, she should envy the birds their wings to fly with. 'And oh, that some one would allow me' (how tender are these words of hers!) 'to go as far as India, to take those Indian children and instruct them in our holy Faith, so that Jesus should possess their souls, and they Him!' And then going on to speak of infidels in general, she said: 'If I could I would put all of them together in the bosom of the Church, and then I should wish that she would breathe on them, purge them from all their infidelity, regenerate them, make them her children, place them at her sweet breasts, and suckle them with the milk of the Holy Sacraments. Oh, how well she would nourish them at her breast! Oh, how willingly I would do this if I could!'

Reflecting on the harm that was being done by the spread of heresies, she said: 'Ah, our souls ought to be always moaning, like turtle doves, and weeping over the blindness of heretics!' And when she thought how the faith of Catholics had grown cold, she said: 'Diffuse it, O Word! Diffuse it living and ardent in the hearts of Thy faithful, warmed and inflamed in the furnace of Thy heart, of Thy infinite charity; so that their faith may be in conformity with their works, and their works in conformity with the Faith! Thy Faith goes the way of the sun. It rises in one place, and sets in another; it appears here, and disappears there. And what marks the setting of this sun? The ever-increasing shadows of sin.' And again, while praying for the conversion of sinners, she said: 'Grant this, not to me, for I am too presumptuous, but to Thine own Blood. Thou canst not be wanting to Thyself. Grant it, O Word, to Thine own Blood.' This ardent zeal for the conversion of souls she wished to transfuse into every one, and therefore she was continually telling the nuns confided to her care that they should be always asking God for souls. 'Let us ask for as many' (as she expressed it) 'as the steps we walk through the convent—as many as the words we recite in the Office.' Her works, as far as her position as a nun would allow, were equal to the ardour of her affection; so that the author of her life has been able to fill fourteen chapters (from xcvii. to cxi.) with evidences of her zeal for the salvation of souls. She had omitted nothing—neither disciplines, nor fastings, nor prolonged prayers, nor reproofs. Sometimes she passed whole months in penance for some sinner who had been recommended to her.

This example should suffice without any other argument; and all truly devout souls will easily be convinced that zeal for the salvation of souls is a virtue which must necessarily be found in every one who feels a tender love for the Divine Blood that redeemed them. 'Qui non zelat non amat,'—'He who has no zeal has no love,' said St. Augustine.

And, besides, we should calculate the immense advantage of it to ourselves, if there were no other than this, that the souls we have helped to save can never be forgetful of us. The same saint, in that ecstasy during which she contemplated St. Aloysius Gonzaga in Heaven, saw, amongst other things, that he was praying warmly for those who on earth had given him spiritual help ; and transported out of herself as she was, she said,' I too desire to labour at helping souls, so that if any of them go to Heaven they may pray for me, as Aloysius does for those who helped him on earth.'

ON THE CAUSES AND EFFECTS OF TRIBULATION.

BY THE BLESSED HENRY SUSO.

From the Dialogue between the Eternal Wisdom and the Soul.

WISDOM. They show little understanding who repine and grumble at every affliction ; for, indeed, My paternal chastisement proceeds from My very great love, and really is sweet and beneficent ; so that he from whom it is never absent may reasonably think himself happy. His affliction does not proceed from any rigour or sharpness on My part, but from My most tender and benign love towards him ; and I wish this to be understood of every cross and tribulation whatsoever, whether freely encountered or otherwise. As a rule, necessity becomes a virtue in the latter case, provided that he who suffers the cross does not wish to be exempt from it, contrary to My designs, and provided that he refer his sufferings, with amiable and patient humility, to My eternal honour. The more these sufferings are in union with love and a ready will, the nobler it is, the more acceptable to Me. Listen, therefore, attentively, whilst I discourse a little more at length about these afflictions. Imprint My words on thine heart, keep them as a mark before thine eyes ; and be sure of this : I dwell in a pure soul, as in a paradise of delights ; and that is why I cannot bear to see its affections attracted to anything in this world.

It has a natural inclination to pernicious pleasure; therefore I hedge its paths with thorns and, whether it be willing or unwilling, bar the road with adversity, so that it may not escape even the least. I strew all its ways with affliction, in order that its happiness may be set on Me alone. Believe Me, if all the joys of earth were concentrated in one single soul, that soul could not even then comprehend the least of the rewards which those will enjoy in the eternal country as a recompense for every cross, however small, borne here below for love of Me.

The Soul. It cannot be denied, O Lord, that afflictions are very salutary, provided they be not too excessive, unusual and distressing. But Thou, Lord, who alone knowest every hidden thing, and didst create everything in number, weight, and measure, —Thou seest very well that my sorrows pass all bounds, and are too much for my strength. Really I know not that there exists in the world a person more afflicted than myself, nor do I know how I am to bear up against such trials. For, indeed, if I had to deal with ordinary sorrows, O Lord, I would endure them willingly; but these extraordinary crosses, which Thou alone canst understand, so pierce the inmost recesses of soul and mind, that I do not see how I can bear them.

Wisdom. Every sick person thinks his own infirmity the worst, and every one who is thirsty imagines that no one is more miserable than himself. If I had afflicted thee differently, thou wouldst say just what thou sayest now. Within My arms, then, do thou be bravely resigned to whatsoever calamity it may be My Will that thou shouldst suffer, without excepting this or that trial. Knowest thou not that I always do what is best for thee, better than thou couldst do it? Thou knowest very well that I am the Eternal Wisdom; that I alone perfectly know what is most advantageous for thee. Experience must, by this time, have made thee aware that when the trials I send are profitably used, they aim more closely at perfection, go deeper, and advance the soul towards union with God more rapidly than all the means that people choose of their own accord. Why, then, dost thou lament? Why dost thou not rather say, 'Do with me, O most benign Father, what pleases Thee best'?

The Soul. O Lord, this is easily said; but the trials I have to endure are very hard to bear, by reason of their causing such excessive pain.

Wisdom. If the cross gave no pain it would not be a cross; and as nothing is more tormenting than the cross, so nothing more delightful, more desirable, than to have borne it. Crosses and afflictions give pain for a short time, but bring lasting contentment. Those to whom it is a torment and a weariness find it very painful; but those who bear it patiently feel it less. Certainly, if thou didst always abound in spiritual sweetness and the delights of Divine consolation, so as to be quite dissolved in sweetness by that heavenly dew, thou wouldst not have as much merit, nor would it be as acceptable to Me, nor should I be bound by it, and, in a certain sense, made thy debtor, as I am by the crosses and afflictions and mental dryness which thou dost endure from Me with love and self-abandonment. It is easier for ten people to fall away while in a state of tranquillity and enjoyment than for one to be in danger of doing so while constantly in trouble and affliction. Wert thou the most perfect astronomer in the world, couldst thou speak and discourse concerning God as copiously and as elegantly as if thou hadst the speech of all angels and all men—in short, didst thou alone know more than all the literary and scientific men in the world, all this would not profit thee, in respect of a pious and holy life, as much as being resigned to the Divine Will in every affliction; for those sciences are common to the good and the bad, but this is a property of the elect. Oh, if any one could weigh time and eternity with exactness, such a person would certainly prefer to burn for one hundred years in a furnace rather than be deprived of the very smallest recompense reserved for him in Heaven on account of some very slight tribulation; for the one ends at last, the other never.

The Soul. All these things that Thou recallest to my mind, O most benign Jesus, are to an afflicted heart like the sweet sounds of harp-music. Certainly, O Lord, I should willingly bear my crosses, and would not wish to be without them, if I could hear such pleasant words all the while.

Wisdom. Listen now attentively to the sweet melody and the pleasing sound of the well-tuned harp. Observe how pleasantly it echoes on thine ears, and how sweetly it rejoices them. Afflictions and troubles are despised by the world; but by Me they are most highly esteemed. They extinguish My anger, gain My grace and friendship, make a man worthy of My love by rendering him like Myself. Affliction causes the earthly man to become heavenly, alienates him from the world, makes him My familiar friend and servant. It diminishes the number of his friends, certainly; but it increases My grace, and is the sure, the shortest way to Heaven. Believe Me, if men fully understood the utility of tribulation, there is no doubt that they would accept it as a most signal favour from God. Oh, how many who were hurrying to perdition, and would have slept an eternal sleep, have been aroused by affliction to lead a better life! Oh, how many are kept in restraint by crosses and afflictions, like wild beasts shut up in their cages, who, were they set free, would at once rush into manifest danger of eternal damnation! Affliction saves a man from great and ruinous falls, makes him know himself, be recollected, and keep faith with his neighbour. It preserves his humility, teaches him patience, and finally brings him the crown of eternal beatitude. Thou canst hardly find any one who does not derive some advantage from affliction and from the fire of adversity, whether he be still immersed in sin or whether he have already begun to amend, be he advancing towards perfection, or be he even perfect. Fire purges iron, purifies gold, and shapes it into precious necklaces; but affliction takes off the burden of sin, diminishes the pains of purgatory, drives away temptations, keeps away vices, renews the spirit, gives true hope, purges the conscience, and steadies and elevates the mind. Tribulation is a useful beverage, a herb more salutary than all the herbs of Paradise: it chastens the body, that will soon dissolve in corruption, but restores the soul, which is immeasurably more noble, and will live for ever. As the gentle dews of flowery May refresh the vermilion leaves of the rose, tribulation restores the soul and makes it fruitful, filling the mind with wisdom and making it habitual. What can he possibly know who has had no experience of affliction and temptations? Tribulation is a rod that is wielded in love, a paternal chastisement reserved for My elect. It draws a man on, and, whether he will or no, forces him towards God. To one who is cheerful in adversity everything turns out for the best. Prosperity and adversity are profitable to him; friends and enemies equally useful. Oh, how often thou thyself hast put thine adversaries to flight, and deprived them of all power, by bearing adversity with a cheerful and thanksgiving heart! In truth, I had rather make temptations and troubles arise out of nothing than leave My friends without crosses; for through suffering all virtues become solid, a man is ennobled by enduring it, his neighbour is ready to do better, and God is the more glorified. Patience in trouble is a living victim and most pleasing odour of most excellent balsam before My Divine Majesty, and it fills all the heavenly court with great admiration. Never has even the bravest soldier or knight, in single combat with his enemy, attracted the eyes and minds of the spectators as much as he who bears tribulation well attracts the observation of all the blessed. It is a more excellent thing to be patient in adversity than to raise the dead or work other miracles. Affliction is a narrow but direct road to the gates of Heaven. It raises a man to fellowship with the martyrs, and is triumphantly victorious over every foe. It gives the soul a gold and purple garment, woven crowns and rose garlands, and a sceptre of verdant palms. It is like a most precious jewel in the necklace of a graceful young virgin. Melodiously and with freedom of spirit affliction sings in Paradise a new song, which even the angels cannot sing, because they never had experience of any trouble. In short, this world calls afflicted people miserable, but I call them happy, because I have chosen them for Myself.

The Soul. Well do I see, O Lord, that Thou art

the Eternal Wisdom; for Thou showest forth the truth so clearly that it is no longer possible to have any doubts about it. No wonder they to whom Thou dost thus show the advantages of trouble are able to bear them. Certainly, O Lord, Thy sweet words have, I confess it, worked such a change in me, that for the future every cross and vexation will seem much more tolerable and even pleasant. O Lord God, my most clement Father, behold me prostrate before Thee. From my inmost heart I praise and thank Thee for all the afflictions that torment me now, and also for those that are past, however bitter and wearisome, to which I once felt a great repugnance, because it appeared to me that they indicated Thine anger and aversion on Thy part.

Wisdom. But what opinion hast thou now?

The Soul. Now, O Lord, as I fix mine eyes lovingly on Thee, I am quite convinced that all those sharp and bitter crosses with which Thou in Thy paternal benignity hast tried me, the mere contemplation of which, when I was oppressed by them, alarmed my friends—and they were no ordinary ones, were but as the sweet dew of flowery spring.

TRIBULATION IS A SIGN OF PREDESTINATION.

ST. GERTRUDE, VIRGIN.

As the ring is the sign of marriage, so is adversity, both corporal and spiritual, patiently borne for the love of God, a most true pledge of Divine election, and is like a marriage of the soul with God.

THE END.

www.ingramcontent.com/pod-product-compliance
Lightning Source LLC
Chambersburg PA
CBHW020911230426
43666CB00008B/1403